On Trust

Increasing the Effectiveness of Charity Trustees and Management Committees

Report of the NCVO/Charity Commission
Working Party on Trustee Training
Chair: Winifred Tumim

Published by
NCVO Publications (incorporating Bedford Square Press)
imprint of the
National Council for Voluntary Organisations
8 Regent's Wharf, All Saints Street, London N1 9RL

First published 1992

Typeset by Contour Typesetters, Southall, London
Printed in Great Britain by Biddles Ltd, Guildford, Surrey
Cover printed by The Heyford Press, Northampton

ISBN 0 7199 1361 6

Contents

Foreword

Liberty needs the manifold associations of civil society, including the voluntary organisations through which citizens express their interests and concerns without calling on the state. The British tradition of voluntary action is a model for Europe, and in recent years we have seen a heightened awareness of its contibution. Unfortunately, this has not always gone hand in hand with an increased readiness on the part of individuals and companies to support charities, though an impressive number of people have given both time and money to their various causes. Many of them, and especially those who have given their time, will have made a discovery which is not surprising though it remains a little discouraging: it is not all that easy to translate given intentions into effective action. Between our intentions and their realisation there stands a world of difficult detail. Issues of law, of finance and of management have to be resolved. Unless they are resolved in a satisfactory manner, good intentions remain mere straws in the wind, and if they are not resolved properly, the whole cause is put in jeopardy. For charity and effective voluntary action depend on trust, the trust of those who are asked for their support, and the trust of the community at large in the associations and organisations which are created.

Such trust is not a matter of course. It requires the highest moral standards on the part of those involved in voluntary work, but it also requires knowledge. It is, therefore, appropriate that the National Council for Voluntary Organisations (NCVO) and the Charity Commission should have set up a working party to try and spell out what it takes to be a trustee, and more generally to engage in charitable work. This report will make a major contribution towards justifying public trust in voluntary action and thus preserving the autonomy which makes up our civil society. I recommend it warmly to all who are, or intending to be, concerned with voluntary and charitable work.

Sir Ralf Dahrendorf KBE FBA

Preface

The voluntary sector gives organisational expression to an exceedingly wide range of concerns, aspirations and passions to be found in a free society, be they social, environmental, religious, educational or aesthetic. Even were the state to make considerably more resources available to publicly funded institutions the particular claims of disadvantaged groups and unpopular causes would continue to stir the imagination of concerned individuals. Such altruistic impulses can only find expression in a free society in which organisations have independence of action. As Beveridge put it: 'The vigour and abundance of voluntary action . . . individually or in association with other citizens for bettering one's own life and that of one's fellows are the distinguishing marks of a free society.'

The voluntary sector in the 1990s is growing and dynamic. Each year about 4,000 charities are registered and the sector's current turnover is of the order of £17 billion a year – over 3 per cent of the Gross Domestic Product and greater than the turnover of the agricultural sector. Across the political divide there has been an ideological shift from 'stateism' to a mixed economy of welfare in which the special characteristics and values of voluntary action are increasingly acknowledged. These characteristics include:

- commitment to a common charitable bond or mission;
- closeness to the consumer, whether geographically or by virtue of special expertise and personal experience;
- ability to advocate on behalf of particular groups and interests;
- capacity to innovate and respond to unmet needs quickly and flexibly; and
- enterprise and willingness to take considered risks.

In addition, voluntary action contributes to the healthy functioning of a democratic society by empowering individuals and enabling them to become active citizens through participating in the governance of voluntary bodies large and small.

The growth in voluntary action poses important challenges to voluntary organisations and raises questions concerning their governance and accountability. These issues were recognised in the Nathan report on 'Effectiveness and the Voluntary Sector' which emphasised that trustees hold the ultimate power and authority in relation to all aspects of the work of a voluntary organisation, and argued strongly that, to be effective, trustees need to be well informed, supported, encouraged – in a word, trained. The report also pointed out the inadequacy of present arrangements for the guidance and training of trustees and recommended that training should become widely recognised.

Both NCVO and the Charity Commission took this recommendation very seriously and accordingly invited me to chair this Working Party to consider the whole issue. The Working Party's deliberations have coincided with the passage of the Charities Act 1992 and, taken with the new statutory framework, we believe that our recommendations could have a far-reaching impact on voluntary organisations and significantly enhance the public's confidence in the sector as a whole.

We are particularly concerned with charity trustees defined by the Charities Act 1960. (n.b. The definitions of terms used in this report are contained in a glossary on p. 105.) We also have a far wider concern with other forms of trusteeship and with those people involved in the management committees of other not-for-profit, independent voluntary organisations set up for community benefit. Our report, therefore, covers the whole range of organisations, from small local groups run wholly by volunteers – such as a local self-help group for a particular ethnic minority or a local branch of the Women's Institute – to multi-million-pound organisations such as the National Trust with many hundreds of paid staff. A body of people with ultimate legal responsibility in relation to all aspects of a voluntary organisation, charitable or otherwise, is variously known as the management committee, the board of trustees, the executive committee or some similar term. To avoid confusion in the text of the report we refer to all voluntary committees with a governance role as the Committee. In the case studies, we have used the terminology used by the organisations themselves. Where American experience is cited, we have used Board for this is the term in use in America. To discharge their role effectively, Committees need to know their

2

legal and managerial responsibilities, and in this report we have tried to chart the areas with which they should be concerned.

We have not hidden present weakness, but our contacts have shown a widespread desire for improvement. Indeed, we have been impressed by the many charities who are already addressing these issues and they have provided us with many examples of best practice. Our analysis and recommendations have been informed by a substantial body of evidence backed up by the findings of specially commissioned research into trustees' perception of their own training needs.

Our report is based on the premise that charities should regulate themselves in an open and publicly accountable way. Trustees must therefore take responsibility individually for the effective oversight of their own organisation, and be encouraged to seek relevant information and training. But action is also needed by other agencies, such as the Charity Commission and NCVO, central and local government, the private sector, local development agencies and funding bodies. We have put forward a number of practical recommendations which we commend to individual trustees, voluntary organisations and all those with a stake in seeing a trusted and flourishing voluntary sector.

Winifred Tumim OBE
Chair of the Working Party

The Working Party's approach

The Working Party was established by NCVO and the Charity Commission in March 1991.

Members of the Working Party have served in an individual capacity, rather than formally representing their organisations. In addition to being drawn from a range of relevant disciplines (law, accountancy, fundraising, management), we also, between us, have experience of both national and local voluntary action, in urban and rural areas.

We have received oral and written evidence from over 70 organisations and individuals (see Appendix 1). Those giving evidence have come from many different parts of the voluntary sector, including housing, social welfare, museums, community enterprise, overseas aid and the environment. They have included community organisations, as well as national charities; self-help groups as well as federations; Black and ethnic minority groups as well as rural groups; companies as well as unincorporated bodies; intermediary bodies as well as service providers. We have heard from a number of trainers and consultants, from central and local government and from trusts and foundations.

We have also commissioned our own telephone survey of a sample of 221 trustees of national and local charities. The results of this survey are published in full in *Trustee Training and Support Needs*, and we have drawn on its findings throughout our work.

Inevitably, there are some parts of the voluntary sector we have not involved. Despite this, we believe our recommendations will still be relevant to all those who are trustees of voluntary organisations of any kind.

In addition to taking evidence and carrying out a survey, we have consulted with voluntary organisations and training providers at different stages of our work. We met with the seven local projects involved in the Advancing Good Management Scheme based at NCVO and we held a meeting and discussed our progress at NCVO's AGM. We also circulated our draft recommendations to all those who gave evidence or were known to have an interest in our work (over 170 people in all) and held a consultative meeting with them. As far as possible our report has taken account of their helpful comments.

NCVO's brief, and therefore the Working Party's brief, only covers England. We are pleased that the Northern Ireland Council of Voluntary Action, Scottish Council for Voluntary Organisations and Wales Council for Voluntary Action have welcomed the report, and hope that it will be useful to voluntary organisations in other parts of the United Kingdom.

Acknowledgements

First I should like to thank my colleagues on the Working Party, especially my vice-chair Diane Yeo, for all the work they have put into the production of this report. We have met 10 times and had a number of consultative meetings. Working Party members have also undertaken interviews and contributed papers. It really has been a *working* party.

Secondly thanks are due to all those who have given evidence, whether orally or in writing; those who have attended consultative meetings; and those who have commented on our draft recommendations. Without their help, we would not have been able to produce our report.

I would also like to acknowledge the financial support of the Hilden Trust, whose generous grant has helped meet the Working Party's costs including commissioning particular pieces of research. The Nuffield Foundation and the Home Office (Voluntary Services Unit) also contributed towards the cost of our survey.

Finally, all the members of the Working Party would like to thank NCVO and in particular Richard Gutch and Tim Dartington, who have serviced the Working Party and drafted the report.

Winifred Tumim

Membership and terms of reference of the Working Party

Chair: Winifred Tumim, Chair of Royal National Institute for the Deaf

Vice Chair: Diane Yeo, Charity Commissioner

Members:

Pesh Framjee, BDO Binder Hamlyn

Sir Reay Geddes, President of Charities Aid Foundation

Valerie Gillespie, Former Vice-Chair of Action with Communities in Rural England

Robert Hazell, Director of Nuffield Foundation

Stephen Lee, Director of Institute of Charity Fundraising Managers

Daniel Levy, Consultant

Fiona Middleton, Partner in Bates, Wells & Braithwaite

Francis Plowden, Partner in Coopers and Lybrand Deloitte

Usha Prashar, Former Director of NCVO

Adrian Randall, Chair of Charity Finance Directors Group

Daphne Statham, Chair of National Association of Councils for Voluntary Service

Michel Syrett, Trustee of Manic Depression Fellowship

Charles Woodd, Director of National Federation of Community Organisations

Observer: Roger Watkins, Home Office

Notes:

- Members of the Working Party serve in an individual capacity and are not formally representing their organisations.
- All members of the Working Party are also trustees of one or more bodies.
- The Working Party has been serviced by Richard Gutch and Tim Dartington (NCV0).

Terms of reference

To determine what training and support for trustees are needed. The Working Party will review the need for training, assess current and emerging provision to determine its suitability, identify gaps in provision, take steps to fill them, and identify the most appropriate ways of promoting training provision for trustees.

Summary

BACKGROUND

In March 1991 NCV0 and the Charity Commission established a working party on trustee training. Its terms of reference and membership are on p. 6.

APPROACH

The Working Party has received oral and written evidence from over 70 organisations and individuals (see Appendix 1). It also commissioned a telephone survey of a sample of 221 trustees of national and local charities.

The Working Party has adopted a broad interpretation of both trustees and training. Although we emphasise throughout our report the particular legal responsibilities of charity trustees, much of what we have to say is equally relevant to the members of management committees of voluntary organisations that are not registered charities or do not have charitable objects, as well as to branch committees within national charities. Therefore, throughout our report and recommendations, references to trustees should be taken to include other management committee members, except where we are referring to the specific legal responsibilities of charity trustees. Likewise references to charities should be taken to include voluntary organisations, with the same proviso as above.

Similarly we are not just concerned with a narrow concept of training, traditionally delivered through courses, but rather with the whole range of advice and support which trustees need to be effective in their role. We have also examined wider organisational factors, such as recruitment, induction and committee arrangements, which can have such a significant impact on the effectiveness of trustees.

NEED

Many voluntary organisations have to grapple with the problems of managing growth and decline and with the emerging 'contract culture'. There is an increasing emphasis on making voluntary organisations accountable both to users and funders. Trustees have to function within a complex legal framework and new legislation affecting the work of charities and voluntary organisations.

We believe therefore that the need for trustee training is greater than ever – and is likely to grow further. There are approximately one million trustees in the UK and up to three million members of management committees. Between them they are responsible for £17 billion per annum, over 200,000 paid staff and over 23 million volunteers. At present much of the training available for them is inaccessible, inappropriate or ignored.

SCOPE

NCVO's brief, and therefore the Working Party's brief, only covers England. We anticipate, however, that most of the recommendations will be equally relevant to Northern Ireland, Scotland and Wales once allowance has been made for different institutional and legal arrangements. We are therefore discussing how best to take this matter forward with the Northern Ireland Council of Voluntary Action, Scottish Council for Voluntary Organisations and Wales Council for Voluntary Action.

Provision of advice, support and training must also take account of the many different kinds of organisation – and trustee – we are dealing with. The needs of the trustees of the National Trust and Oxfam will be very different from the needs of smaller charities, most of whom have no paid staff at all.

In our analysis we have distinguished between:

- organisations with no staff, paid or unpaid, where the work of the organisation falls to its own trustees;
- organisations with a few staff, paid or unpaid; and
- organisations with significant numbers of staff, ranging from medium-sized charities to the large national service-based organisations with many hundreds of staff.

We also distinguish between organisations without significant capital assets and those which own and manage property and/or sizeable investments.

The trustees of each of these types of organisation – or combination of types – are likely to be faced with different kinds of challenges and responsibilities.

CONTEXT

Involvement as a trustee is an important aspect of active citizenship which not only brings benefits to society but also enables individuals to develop and gain new skills and interests.

Yet, it is clear from our own survey, and other sources, that currently trustees are not representative of society as a whole. Typically, they are over 45, from professional backgrounds, white, and more likely to be male. People from Black and ethnic minority communities are under-represented, while white working class people would seem to play very little part in the governance of charity.

FRAMEWORK FOR ACTION

We have learned much from the experience of other countries, such as the USA, and from other related fields, such as school governing bodies, local authority councillors and non-executive directors of companies.

Our aim throughout has been to achieve action which will increase the effectiveness of trustees. In order to do this we have developed a framework for action comprising:

(a) *The content and approach* of any advice, support and training for trustees;
(b) Action by *organisations* to support their trustees;
(c) Action by *agencies* providing advice and support;
(d) Action by *government and other funders*; and
(e) Action by *individual* trustees.

Our recommendations have been developed within this framework.

RESPONSIBILITIES

Trustees themselves have the prime responsibility for ensuring high standards rather than having them imposed by external or statutory enforcement agencies. Nevertheless, a number of different agencies have important roles in helping trustees discharge these responsibilities effectively, especially since many trustees are unaware of their position and responsibilities.

Voluntary organisations themselves are in the best position to identify their own trustees' needs and take appropriate action. But where trustees are unaware of their position and responsibilities, or if an organisation has unpaid staff, they will need to be reminded of their responsibilities by the Charity Commission and other agencies. Voluntary organisations also need advice on how best to support their trustees and an appropriate range of training and information needs to be developed. The Charity Commission, NCVO, central and local government, other funders and many other national and local agencies all have a role to play in bringing this about.

We believe that it is important that trustees know where they can go for help and advice; that they have a choice of avenues to pursue; and that provision is tailored to their needs. This is what our recommendations aim to achieve.

Recommendations

CONTENT AND APPROACH

Roles and responsibilities

The roles and responsibilities of charity trustees are wide-ranging, and their particular function will be affected by the size and nature of the charity. They can be summarised under three main headings:

- legal responsibilities, to see that the charity is abiding by its objects and constitution and operating within the constraints of the law;
- financial responsibilities, to see that any monies and property are held in trust for the beneficiaries of the charity and that all financial matters are properly and effectively managed; and
- managerial responsibilities including the appointment of and contractual relationships with staff (including volunteers), ensuring accountability to funders, users and members; representing the view of the organisation on issues relating to the interests of the organisation; and strategic planning including the identification of the mission of the organisation, maintenance of values and evaluation of the organisation's activities.

These roles and responsibilities also apply (albeit not within the framework of charity law) to the members of management committees of voluntary organisations which are not charities.

We were concerned to learn from our survey of charitable organisations how few (one in three) respondents actually knew they were charity trustees.

The chair, treasurer and other honorary officers of voluntary organisations have particular roles and responsibilities, which we believe need to be more explicitly addressed in the development of future training provision. The chair, in particular, has a responsibility for the overall governance of the organisation and for liaison with the senior staff member.

WE THEREFORE RECOMMEND THAT

1 Resource material and training provision for trustees should clearly state their main roles and responsibilities, highlighting the particular roles and responsibilities of the chair, treasurer and other honorary officers.

What trustees need to know

We recognise that what trustees need to know depends partly on the type of organisation they are involved in. Nevertheless, there are certain common areas of knowledge and competence which all trustees need to have. Some will need more detailed and greater depth of knowledge than others, but all will need a basic awareness and familiarity with these subject areas.

WE THEREFORE RECOMMEND THAT

2 Advice, support and training for trustees should cover the following eight subject areas:
  - organisational context;
  - legal responsibilities;
  - financial responsibilities;
  - personnel responsibilities, where relevant;
  - property responsibilities, where relevant;
  - strategic planning and evaluation;
  - strategic management and accountability; and
  - working structures and relationships.
These should cover the full range of their role and responsibilities and not be limited to their legal responsibilities.

A broad approach to training

We think it is important to adopt a broad approach to the training of trustees in terms of both content and delivery. Those involved in organising training should recognise that an expressed need for training may often encompass a further need for consultation and advice. It is also important to recognise that paid staff need training in how to work effectively with trustees.

WE THEREFORE RECOMMEND THAT

3 Training courses should be particularly targeted at inexperienced trustees and lead at least to a certificate of attendance and, where possible, to some form of accreditation of courses.
4 Training provision should be:
 - assessed for its accessibility in terms of time, cost and familiarity of language and approach; and
 - fully accessible, for example through the provision of interpreters at meetings, including sign language interpreters for deaf people, sub-titles on videos, and translation into other languages, as required.
5 Meetings of the Committee should be seen as opportunities for learning, and training elements and review processes built into the annual cycle of meetings.

Mechanisms

We have looked carefully at the range of mechanisms needed to deliver advice, support and training. No one mechanism will be sufficient on its own, but taken together, over time, we believe they would have a significant impact in increasing the effectiveness of trustees. Responsibilities for implementing these mechanisms are discussed under Recommendations 18–40.

WE THEREFORE RECOMMEND THAT

6 A range of different training courses should be developed to meet the needs of different kinds of organisation, for example community organisations with no staff, large national charities and organisations with significant capital assets. Joint training of trustees and staff should be included as part of any programme for organisations employing staff.
7 Distance learning initiatives, such as the Open University's new voluntary sector management course, need to be developed further and made accessible to the full range of trustees.
8 A general information pack for trustees and their organisations should be produced in a form which can then be adapted and added to by particular networks or individual voluntary organisations. The core content of the information pack should include sections on:

 - recruitment of trustees;
 - induction of trustees;
 - information to be provided to trustees;
 - the roles and responsibilities of trustees;
 - the questions trustees should be asking;
 - the critical issues trustees should be monitoring;
 - relationships with staff, where relevant;
 - advice on growth and contraction of the organisation;
 - criteria for assessing the provision of advice, support and training; and
 - competencies for trustees.
9 A development unit for trustee support services should be established to encourage and co-ordinate the development of a wide range of advice, support and training for trustees by other agencies (see Recommendation 24).

HOW ORGANISATIONS CAN SUPPORT THEIR TRUSTEES

Responsibilities

We believe that the prime responsibility for ensuring that appropriate advice, support and training of trustees takes place rests with the organisation itself.

WE THEREFORE RECOMMEND THAT

10 The senior staff member, or, where there are no paid staff, the chair, should:
 - ensure that the Committee considers the issue of training of trustees;
 - implement whatever is agreed; and
 - ensure that the organisation budgets for training of trustees in the same way as for other activities.

Recruitment

The trustees of charities are chosen in different ways. Some are appointed, others are elected by geographical or representative constituencies, while yet others are chosen by open election. Good practice for organisations will be to an extent governed by these differences. Nevertheless all charities need to consider what kind of skills and experience they are seeking in their trustees. Equal opportunity considerations should also be taken into account. When appropriate, the same principles involved in recruiting paid staff should be applied to recruiting trustees.

It is clear from our survey and other evidence presented to us that most of these procedures are not currently followed. This is clearly part (but only part) of the reason trustees are so unrepresentative of the population as a whole in terms of age, class, gender, race, disability and other characteristics.

WE THEREFORE RECOMMEND THAT

11 Charities should develop clear guidelines on what they expect of their trustees, both individually and collectively. These should include the expected time commitment, and 'job descriptions' for the chair, treasurer, other honorary officers, and ordinary members of the Committee (which should be complementary to those of the staff).

12 Charities should have a policy for the composition, recruitment and appointment of their Committee, and an equal opportunities policy covering both their services and the recruitment and appointment of their staff and Committee.

Induction

Induction, with adequate time for discussion between new trustees, staff and experienced trustees, was identified as a vital need by the majority of respondents to our survey, yet only just over one trustee in five had been through a recognisable induction process. Roughly the same number again spoke of an informal induction system.

WE THEREFORE RECOMMEND THAT

13 All charities give urgent attention to their induction arrangements for trustees, developing an induction policy and procedures including briefing meetings and the provision of an information pack, including:

- an up-to-date list of trustees of the charity (distinguishing, where necessary, between charity trustees and holding trustees – and with an explanation of the difference);
- an up-to-date list of any other committees or advisory groups, which might have an influence on the management or supervision of the workers of the organisation;
- an organisation chart and list of key staff, with job titles and a clear indication of their responsibilities;
- a statement of the responsibilities, where relevant,

of non-executive directors of companies limited by guarantee;
- a statement of the responsibilities of trustees; this should include essential information from the Charity Commission;
- a statement of the constitution of the organisation, clearly describing the legal status, charitable objectives, and relevant information on the appointment or election of trustees; and
- the organisation's annual report and accounts.

The information pack should provide, or be an opportunity to discuss, a mission statement; include a statement of current objectives, and policies to achieve them; indicate any problems to be overcome; and describe external relations (including sources of funding and any conditions attached to funds).

This information pack should build on the core material referred to in Recommendation 8.

Continuing support

Although good induction procedures are a prerequisite for effective trusteeship, they should not be the sum total of the organisation's trustee training efforts – yet too often they are. There is also a need for continuing advice, support and training based on an assessment of need.

WE THEREFORE RECOMMEND THAT

14 Charities should carry out regular assessments of the training needs of their trustees and ensure that there is a rolling programme of advice, support and training for them within the resources available.

Reinforcement and review

Our survey showed that only one trustee in three actually knew they were a charity trustee. Although this is partly a problem of terminology, we believe it reflects a wider problem, namely that the roles and responsibilities of trustees are not sufficiently central and explicit within the work of many charities. Trustees do not think of themselves as trustees because their organisations often do not think of them as trustees either.

15 Annual reports and other relevant publications should clearly identify trustees as trustees with a statement of the action that the charities have taken to provide training for both trustees and paid staff.

16 Charities should consider appropriate ways of reinforcing the status and responsibilities of their trustees, for example through addressing them as 'trustees' in correspondence.

17 Charities should hold at least one meeting annually, at which trustees review and evaluate the overall work of the organisation and set objectives for it and for themselves.

ACTION BY AGENCIES PROVIDING ADVICE AND SUPPORT

The Charity Commission

We believe that the Charity Commission has a continuing role to play in the provision of advice, support and training for trustees.

WE THEREFORE RECOMMEND THAT

18 The Charity Commission should produce a new basic leaflet aimed at potential and existing trustees, outlining in very clear, simple terms their responsibilities and roles. This leaflet should aim to provide all potential and existing trustees with essential introductory information, from which they could then go on to look at the range of existing booklets already available from the Charity Commission.

19 The leaflet should be sent to all charities with the new annual charity return in sufficient quantities for each trustee to have one. The Charity Commission should also send it to any new or potential trustees who come to its notice and copies should be available at other outlets, such as local libraries, local development agencies and citizen advice bureaux. It should also be sent to organisations which supply large numbers of trustees, such as local authorities and companies, and be produced in minority ethnic languages, in braille and on tape.

20 The Charity Commission should continue to keep under review all its current explanatory leaflets to ensure that they are written in as accessible a manner as possible, and expand its range of advice by issuing guidance on:

- the potential duplication of activities between charities;
- appropriate sizes of Committees;
- terms of office for trustees;
- mergers of existing charities; and
- the winding up of charities.

The Charity Commission should consult with NCVO and other umbrella bodies before finalising the content of this new guidance.

21 The Charity Commission should play a leading role within government in trying to persuade government, local authorities and other funders to invest in improving provision of advice, support and training for trustees.

22 The Charity Commission should convene a standing committee of relevant organisations with NCVO to review the provision of advice, support and training for trustees on an ongoing basis.

National Council for Voluntary Organisations

We believe that there is an urgent need for NCVO, as the main representative body for the voluntary sector in England, to provide a lead within the voluntary sector on the issue of trustee training, working with other development agencies in developing trustee support services, to be delivered nationally and locally through a range of organisations, and in producing the core material for a trustee information pack as well as playing a co-ordinating and enabling role in helping new forms of provision to develop.

NCVO should work with others to develop the costings of the proposals in this report and encourage central and local government, the private sector and charitable trusts to invest in them as appropriate.

Since charity trustees are one of the defining features of the voluntary sector (without whom there would literally be no voluntary sector), it is important that NCVO's work should address their needs and interests.

WE THEREFORE RECOMMEND THAT

23 NCVO should give much higher priority to working with trustees, and particularly their chairs, than it has done hitherto and should take steps to ensure that its work and services are accessible to them. This will have implications for its mailing lists, the type of information it produces and the timing of meetings it organises.

24 NCVO, working with relevant organisations, should establish a development unit for trustee support services which would:

- develop existing advice, support and training, through working with other relevant agencies;
- train trainers and other advisers (including professionals such as solicitors) working with trustees;
- advise other providers on content and approach;
- maintain a data-base of available advice, support and training for trustees;
- publicise sources of advice, support and training for trustees; and
- develop and maintain a network of trustees, particularly focusing on the chairs of charities and of voluntary organisations.

The development unit should maintain a more strategic role in developing provision.

25 NCVO should produce the core material for the information pack referred to in Recommendation 8 and encourage other national networks and charities to add to or adapt it to suit their particular needs.

Other agencies

As we have emphasised above, a wide range of other agencies have an important role to play in the provision of advice, support and training for trustees in addition to the Charity Commission and NCVO.

Within the voluntary sector, generalist development agencies such as the Volunteer Centre UK, the National Association of Councils for Voluntary Service, Action with Communities in Rural England, the National Association of Volunteer Bureaux and the National Federation of Community Organisations all have an important contribution to make. More specialist development agencies such as the Organisation Development Unit for ethnic minorities, the National Alliance of Women's Organisations, the Institute of Charity Fundraising Managers and other specialist networks can help provide advice, support and training for trustees within their membership or constituency. National federations also have an important role in providing advice, support and training to their local members.

A wide range of other trainers, consultants and companies also have a crucial role in developing and delivering appropriate forms of provision.

WE THEREFORE RECOMMEND THAT

26 Generalist and specialist development agencies, federations and networks within the voluntary sector, nationally and locally, should consider how they can best contribute to the provision of advice, support and training for trustees. They should draw on the expertise of consultants and trainers with experience of meeting the needs of trustees. Particular consideration should be given to the need for advice and support to the 40,000 rural grant-giving charities in England.

27 Action Resource Centre and Business in the Community should explore ways of increasing awareness of the voluntary sector among the professions, as well as building on current initiatives for increasing free advice provision.

28 Colleges of further and higher education, education agencies and youth and community organisations should discuss possible initiatives for training trustees with local development agencies such as Councils for Voluntary Service and Rural Community Councils.

29 Other agencies, such as local authorities and companies, should consider whether any of the training they provide for local authority councillors and non-executive directors could, appropriately, be made available to trustees. They should also consider providing those of their own staff who wish to become trustees with appropriate training.

ACTION BY GOVERNMENT AND OTHER FUNDERS

Investment required

Many of those giving evidence or surveyed emphasised the need for more resources. Charities struggling to raise money for their core expenditure are unlikely to spend resources on training for trustees. Generalist and specialist development agencies will need resources to develop the range of provision we have recommended.

Although we accept that resources in themselves will not result in the improvements we are seeking, we do agree that there must be additional investment if progress is to be made. We would also argue that funders have a responsibility to contribute towards this investment.

WE THEREFORE RECOMMEND THAT

30 Funders should increase their investment in the provision of advice, support and training for trustees. Grants and contracts with individual charities and voluntary organisations should allow for expenditure on trustee training.

31 The Voluntary Services Unit in the Home Office should take a lead role in central government in

helping to implement the recommendations of this report and in ensuring a co-ordinated response, including a funding contribution, from central government to the recommendations in this report.

32 Core funding should be increased for national and local development agencies and networks to enable them to develop their provision of trustee training.

Funding relationships

As well as providing resources, funders are well placed to influence the organisations they fund, either directly through funding conditions or, more indirectly, through the relationships they develop with applicants and funded organisations. The recent Efficiency Scrutiny Review into the funding of voluntary organisations by central government recognised the importance of increasing the effectiveness of these funding relationships.

However, it has to be recognised that giving greater priority to developing effective funding relationships also requires additional investment. Funders themselves will need the appropriate staff and expertise.

WE THEREFORE RECOMMEND THAT

33 Funders should ask for details of trustees and try to meet with some of them, as well as with the paid staff. This may often involve funders in having to arrange meetings outside normal office hours.

34 Funders should encourage all trustees to think about their training needs. When providing funding, funders should, where appropriate, separately identify an element for staff and trustee training, and advise the organisations they fund on appropriate sources of advice, support and training for trustees.

35 Funders should, as far as possible, establish mechanisms for monitoring and evaluating the governance of the organisations they fund and, where necessary, require additional trustee training to take place.

ACTION BY INDIVIDUAL TRUSTEES

Whether to become a trustee and performing the role effectively

Although individual charities, their paid staff and national and local agencies all have very important roles to play in helping increase the effectiveness of trustees, ultimately it is trustees themselves who are actually responsible for their own performance. We have therefore examined the potential obstacles facing trustees in performing their role effectively and identified a number of ways in which they can be overcome.

Trustees must consider carefully what is involved in becoming a trustee. Having made the decision to do so, they must take appropriate steps to perform their role effectively.

WE THEREFORE RECOMMEND THAT

36 All potential trustees should ask their charity to provide them with relevant Charity Commission guidance, including the proposed leaflet (see Recommendation 18) and a statement of what is expected of them, including a job description and person specification where they exist, and a copy of the charity's constitution and annual report and accounts.

37 All potential trustees should make a careful assessment of the responsibilities involved in being a trustee, including the commitment of time, beyond what may be needed for attendance at meetings.

38 Trustees should
   – ask for appropriate information to be provided by the organisation;
   – ensure that they receive relevant papers;
   – take appropriate action when they have concerns about the organisation; and
   – voice their concerns to the chair or at Committee, and if necessary make contact with the relevant trustee support services (see Recommendations 24 and 26).

Taking on responsibilities

It is essential that trustees are aware of the responsibilities they are taking on. Although they may delegate the work involved in these responsibilities to paid staff, they cannot delegate or avoid the responsibilities themselves.

WE THEREFORE RECOMMEND THAT

39 Trustees agree to undertake, by signing a statement, that they will discharge their legal, financial and managerial responsibilities. Individual trustees should be encouraged to consider at least once a year whether they are willing to continue as a trustee,

bearing in mind the roles and responsibilities required of them.

40 The chair should have overall responsibility for exercising leadership and ensuring that the Committee functions effectively and for identifying the need for advice, support or training for Committee members.

PART ONE
Understanding the need

1 Trustees – who are they?

DEFINITION

The Charities Act 1960 defines 'charity trustees' as those individuals who are responsible for the general control and management of the charity. As such they have a number of specific legal and other responsiblities, which we describe in more detail in Part Two.

'Holding' or 'Custodian' trustees have the more limited function of holding the assets of the charity (and investments) in safe-keeping. They are not actively involved in the management of these assets but must carry out the instructions of the 'charity trustees' provided the instructions are not in breach of the trusts of the charity. The legal responsibilities of holding or custodian trustees are correspondingly less onerous.

The members of the Committee of a charity, whether known as a board, management or executive committee or otherwise, will be the charity trustees in both an unincorporated association and a company limited by guarantee. There may be people elected to manage a local branch of a charity, where the branch is still formally part of the charity as a whole. Only the charity trustees ultimately bear full legal responsibility for its effective governance and conduct.

Not all voluntary organisations are registered charities. Some may be exempt or excepted charities. Some may have charitable objectives, but may not yet have registered or be obliged to register (although in law they are still charities). Some may have non-charitable objectives, but still fulfil the criteria of being not-for-profit, independent, voluntarily-managed and serving a community benefit. Some may be friendly or provident societies, some may be incorporated and some may be unincorporated associations. All these organisations form part of the wider voluntary sector. All of them will have a group of individuals who have responsibility for the overall management and administration of the organisation, referred to in this report as the Committee.

We are particularly concerned with 'charity trustees', but also have a more general concern with the members of the management committees of charities and other voluntary organisations, many of whom will not be charity trustees. Our concern is for all those who receive in trust resources to be applied for the benefit of others.

NUMBERS

According to the Charity Commission, there are approximately 170,000 registered charities in England and Wales and 80,000 exempt or excepted charities, making 250,000 in total. However, the Commission estimates that approximately 30,000 of these may now be defunct. Assuming an average of about 10 trustees per charity, this would give an estimate of 2.2 million trustees. But according to a survey the Working Party commissioned, 60 per cent of trustees are trustees of at least one other charity, so an estimate of one million seems realistic. Once the Charity Commission's register is fully computerised, it will be possible to be more precise.

The Volunteer Centre UK's 1991 National Survey of Voluntary Activity in the UK is another useful source of information. This showed that 15 per cent of all adults in the UK serve on a Committee of some kind in a voluntary capacity. This covers not only voluntary organisations but also other institutions, such as state schools. The survey also covered Northern Ireland and Scotland, whereas the Charity Commission statistics cover only England and Wales. It indicates that we are potentially talking about up to three million people for whom the issues raised in this report will have some relevance.

HOW DO PEOPLE BECOME TRUSTEES?

The two main methods are selection and election. Generally speaking, trustees are either *appointed* by the other trustees, by the founder, by nomination of a third party or by virtue of their office; or they are *elected* by the charity's members. Some charities use a mixture of these methods.

The people put forward for appointment are likely to have come via a number of possible routes. Some are simply likely to be individuals considered to have professional standing or status which will enhance the reputation of the charity and assist with fundraising. Others may have specialist experience particularly relevant to the work of the charity – for example in medicine, education or social services. Others may have particular skills, for example in fundraising or management, relevant to their role as trustee. All will be expected also to have a commitment to the charity's mission.

If a charity elects its trustees some at least are likely to represent particular constituencies. Some, for example, may be elected by their local branch or region. Others may be elected from the membership of the organisation. Others may represent the users or beneficiaries of the charity.

Some charities' constitutions will specify the different constituencies from which their trustees are to be found. For example, many local charities will have a representative of the local authority as a trustee. In all these cases, the people appointed have to remember that, once they become a trustee, their prime duty is to the charity and not to the constituency.

The chair or the senior staff member of the charity in many cases suggests someone may like to become a trustee or may like to stand for election. The process of selection or election can sometimes look similar.

A charity's constitution should also specify the procedure for reappointing, removing or replacing trustees. In many charities, especially where trustees are not subject to election, the trustees remain in office for as long as they wish.

The same kinds of appointment methods are found in management committees of voluntary organisations which are not charities.

In our survey just under half the trustees described themselves as elected. The majority of these, however, appear to have been elected without opposition. Existing trustees identified and selected prospective trustees before their 'election' onto the Committee. Three out of ten people said they were 'selected', with no election process. Local organisations had a higher proportion of trustees selected in this way than national organisations. In the survey, 8 per cent were nominated and 9 per cent co-opted to the Committee; 3 per cent described themselves as founders of their organisations, and had been trustees ever since. Others were elected as delegates from local or regional groups – a method described as 'coming up through the ranks'. Overall, the dominant method of recruitment was word-of-mouth.

WHY DO PEOPLE BECOME TRUSTEES?

Little is known about why people decide to become trustees. The Volunteer Centre UK is planning to conduct some research into this, and other questions relating to trustees, in 1992. Its qualitative research into 'images, motivation and experiences' of volunteering (conducted in 1990) sheds some light on people's motivations for volunteering generally, but does not specifically explore motivations for becoming a trustee. Interestingly one of its findings was that most people do not view committee membership as a form of volunteering, which they see as being more concerned with the direct provision of a service to an individual.

A survey carried out by CR Consultants, the management consultancy wing of Charity Recruitment, in 1989, included a number of questions about people's motivations for become a trustee:

Why did you become a trustee?

Personally affected by charity's work	29%
Knew someone on the board	21%
Interest	16%
Worked in the field	15%
Prestige	6%

What did you hope to bring to the Board?

Expertise	84%
Knowledge of the field	60%
Contacts	26%
Financial assistance	7%

What kind of expertise did you hope to bring?

Managerial	70%
Financial	40%
Public relations	29%
Professional knowledge	27%
Fundraising experience	23%

By being a board member, what did you hope to influence?

Policy	11%
Focus/aim of charity	60%
Image	44%
Communications	40%
Quality of service	9%

More anecdotal evidence suggests that people have a very wide range of motives for becoming a trustee. Qualitative research carried out by the Volunteer Centre UK in a rural part of Kent suggests that many people tend to drift into becoming a trustee – the Committee chooses them rather than the other way round. People see it more as a chore than an honour and often agree to take it on until someone else comes forward – then stay for much longer than they had expected.

'Active citizens'

The chair of a local tenants association is also a mother of 8 children and grandmother to a further 13. Her appointment came quite suddenly and, as she says, 'Since then it has sort of snowballed.'

She is on call 24 hours a day, but why does she do it?

I think it's just the thought that I can help somebody. It's mostly the old-age pensioners that get to me. If they want a washer on their tap, send for Iris. If somebody's locked out I have to go with a ladder and climb through bedroom windows. But I love the challenge of it, I like to be able to think I can do it.

She feels good relations with the council are crucial. She doesn't let the pressure get to her and has a healthy sense of humour – an essential quality for any association committee chair.

I don't let it worry me, once they've gone from the door. It's only their troubles, and I've done something for them. I force myself not to worry about them. I'm that sort of person, I can laugh at anything.

Other work being done under the Advancing Good Management Scheme, suggests that serving on Committees brings with it a degree of prestige and status for some people, while others find it difficult to get invited in the first place. Similar points were made to us in relation to the Black and ethnic minority voluntary sector, where we were told many people saw involvement in a Committee as a form of career development, which was often denied to them in other walks of life.

Whatever the different motivations or reasons people may have for becoming a trustee, it seems clear to us, from all the evidence that we have received, that most people are not fully aware of the responsibilities they are taking on or the importance of the task they are engaging in.

WHO BECOME TRUSTEES?

Again, little is known about the kind of people who become trustees. The different routes to becoming a trustee mean that a wide range of people become involved. It is quite common to find a successful business person, a local branch member, someone with specialist skills and a service user, all on the same Committee.

The evidence we have, however, is that the majority of trustees are white, middle-aged and middle-class (though not necessarily male).

In our own survey we found men outnumber women three to two at both national and local level. Seventy per cent are over 45; less than one in ten trustees is under 36. Two-thirds of trustees are drawn from professionals and managers; almost no working-class people are trustees. Black and ethnic minorities and disabled people are also under-represented.

These results are scarcely surprising when the methods of recruitment and selection to boards are taken into account. Trustees are selected because they are professionals or managers, and are assumed to have appropriate skills. Relatively few organisations provide training and support to enable untrained or inexperienced people to learn the relevant skills. As one trustee described his board: 'It's a self-perpetuating oligarchy.'

Certainly some of the negative images of volunteering expressed by non-volunteers in the Volunteer Centre UK's survey suggests there is a need to try and change many people's perceptions of trustees. 'Important people who sit on Committees to keep an eye on what's going on' was one person's image of volunteers! There are also clearly a number of barriers discouraging some sections of the community from becoming involved. These include the 'culture' of many Committees, which can sometimes be very unwelcoming to anyone whose background or perspective is different.

Some of those giving evidence criticised the tendency of paid staff from one voluntary organisation to sit on the Committee of another. This is the case in many national voluntary organisations and also occurs in some of the more established or intermediary local organisations such as housing associations, citizens advice bureaux and councils for voluntary service. Some people felt these arrangements were 'incestuous' and out of keeping with the principle of having a *voluntary* Committee. It is important to ensure sufficient involvement of 'lay members' and 'genuine' volunteers.

Many local authority councillors or officers on Committees are unaware that their prime duty is to the charity or voluntary organisation rather than their local authority. Conflicts of interest can arise and the potential legal implications of their involvement are becoming more complex as a result of recent local government legislation. If problems occur, such trustees have the same legal and financial liabilities as their fellows. For many charities, links with the local authority are very important, but it may be preferable for local authority representatives to be non-voting observers rather than Committee members. Accountability for funding can, and should, be ensured in other ways.

There are signs that the kinds of people who become trustees are likely to change in the future. The increasing responsibilities and the contract culture discussed in later chapters are likely to mean that charities and voluntary organisations will be looking for more people with business and professional experience in the future. The signs are that this is already happening in the United States. These developments, including Geneva Johnson's descriptions of 'traditional' and 'new wave' trustees, are discussed in greater depth in Chapter 11.

RECRUITMENT

A number of those giving evidence talked of the increasing difficulties of finding trustees. Demographic trends, working women, rival leisure attractions, screening of volunteers, fear of liabilities and many other factors are all seen as making it harder to attract people to becoming trustees. They will also make it harder to retain existing trustees. One result is that the average age of trustees is increasing, as was demonstrated in the evidence given by the Association of Independent Museums.

It is fair to say that it has probably always been difficult to persuade people to become trustees. On the positive side, as retirement ages reduce and life-spans increase, there is also now great potential for involving more people nearing retirement or recently retired.

We believe that, subject to any legal bar, anyone concerned with working for the benefit of the public or the community, should be free to serve as a charity trustee or a member of a voluntary organisation management committee. At the same time they should also be provided with the necessary advice, support and training to enable them to discharge this role effectively. Being a trustee or member of a management committee is an important aspect of active citizenship which not only benefits society but also enables individuals to develop and gain new skills, interests and satisfaction.

However, it is clear from our own survey, and other sources, that at present trustees are not representative of society as a whole. We believe therefore that more people, from a wider spectrum of society, should be encouraged to become trustees. Although it is outside our terms of reference, we put forward some ideas in our conclusions for further exploration.

We are also aware that there is a very important link between our own recommendations and the need to increase the representativeness of trustees. Unless adequate advice, support and training is provided for trustees, they will continue to be drawn from a predominantly professional background.

LACK OF AWARENESS

One of the more striking findings from our survey is how few trustees realise they *are* trustees. Only one in three of the trustees we surveyed actually knew they were a charity trustee.

This seems partly a problem of language. In organisations with a 'board of trustees', all seemed clear. In organisations with 'management committees', most members seemed unclear whether they were charity trustees. In organisations which had incorporated as limited companies, most respondents saw themselves as directors, but not all were clear whether they were charity trustees as well.

There is clearly a need to find ways of reinforcing the fact that a person is a trustee. He or she is then more likely to take their responsibilities as a trustee seriously.

SUMMARY

In this chapter we have

- defined what we mean by charity trustees and Committees;
- estimated that there are approximately one million charity trustees and up to three million members of Committees of voluntary organisations;
- outlined the different ways in which people become trustees;
- discussed the different reasons why people become trustees;
- noted the difficulties involved in recruiting and retaining trustees;
- noted the unrepresentative nature of trustees as a whole; and
- highlighted the fact that most trustees are unaware that they are trustees.

2 The trustee environment

INTRODUCTION

There are a number of different factors which influence the way in which trustees have to work and the tasks they have to perform. We have identified three main dimensions as being particularly important:

- the type and size of the organisation;
- the employment of staff; and
- how the Committee works.

When considering advice, support and training for trustees, these different variables need to be taken into account.

TYPES OF ORGANISATION

We have distinguished between different types of voluntary organisation, the trustees of which need different support:

- a voluntary self-help group with no paid staff, no previous experience of working as a group. Here the main challenge for the Committee is to develop appropriate structures and ways of enabling the group to function effectively without becoming too formal or losing its original vision.
- organisations with few staff, paid or unpaid. Here the main challenge is to work out appropriate roles for the Committee and staff members and to come to terms with the responsibility of being an employer.
- organisations with significant numbers of staff, ranging from medium-sized charities to the large national service-based organisations with many hundreds of staff. Here the main challenge for trustees is how to develop and maintain good relationships between the Committee and the staff.
- Organisations managing premises and other capital assets. Here trustees need to understand the legal and financial responsibilities involved. (Such organisations may be large or small. Sometimes they will have no paid staff – for example the chair of the Committee may also be the person who opens up for the playgroup in the morning.)

Very often organisations will move rapidly from one phase to another. The most critical time for most organisations is at the point of transition – managing significant funds or employing staff for the first time, managing premises or becoming involved in trading and contractual relations. Each stage represents a particular management challenge, for which the Committee needs to be prepared. As one interviewee stated: 'It is when small groups expand rapidly, acquiring property and employing staff for the first time that the banana skins are most likely to occur.'

Rationale for the structure

Sometimes, when an organisation obtains public funding, or seeks charitable status, it finds a statutory agency effectively imposing on it a particular type of constitution and structure. If the rationale for the structure is not understood and accepted by all concerned, this can be a recipe for confusion and difficulty. We were told that this has often been the case with Black and ethnic minority groups, where more informal ways of working are suddenly replaced with imposed structures. Likewise local authorities often insist that a branch of a national charity is independently constituted and incorporated before agreeing to fund it. Wherever possible, we believe the statutory agencies and advisers involved in this process should try and adopt a developmental rather than an authoritarian approach to these situations.

The purpose of the charity also affects the sort of task facing trustees. Service provision, campaigning, self-help, and local development each bring with them particular types of challenge. Providing services for elderly disabled people, for instance, is very different from the management of a museum or the running of a housing association.

National v local organisation

A critical determinant of the level of advice and support available to trustees is the type of wider organisational structure they relate to.

Federated structures such as those operated by Age Concern England, MIND or the National Association of Citizens Advice Bureaux involve independent local organisations as members being responsible for their own finances and staffing, but with advice and support provided through the national body or through a regional structure of development officers.

Membership bodies such as Arthritis Care and Barnardo's, on the other hand, retain ultimate financial responsibility for their local branches' affairs. Barnardo's recently considered a federated structure but turned the proposal down, partly because of the increased fiduciary responsibilities it would place on local branches.

Some charities such as National Schizophrenia Fellowship encourage particular projects to have independent status, while other branches remain part of the national body. Other voluntary organisations have no national network to relate to, but may be members of their local council for voluntary service or rural community council, which might provide them with appropriate advice and support.

Parochial charities and locally endowed trusts

Research for Wiltshire Community Council and Action with Communities in Rural England has uncovered an estimated 40,000 village charities in England, with over 120,000 trustees and an annual disbursement of £200 million. The aims of the charities range from the presentation of a loaf of bread to the poorest parishioner at Christmas to considerable housing provision and income support to local people in need. Some charities are administered capably and intelligently, some are just ticking over and some have been dormant and unused for many years.

With the help of local advisers, fairly comprehensive lists of these charities have been established in some areas, and help, advice and training seminars offered to trustees. The problems, however, are great: financial constraints limit the time which can be spent in contacting trustees who perhaps are unaware of their trustee status or who are unwilling to pursue their responsibilities any further than attendance at the occasional trustees' meeting. Sometimes the nominated trustees have died and not been replaced.

Experience shows that with sufficient time and effort it is possible to track down these local charities and provide their trustees with appropriate advice and support. Often substantial endowments have been identified which were being insufficiently used. However, national resources for this work have now come to an end despite the continuing need to establish contact with local charities of this kind.

Some organisations may have no immediate source of advice and support locally or nationally. For example, many locally endowed trusts in rural areas are extremely isolated. Similarly, many Black and ethnic minority groups find it difficult to get access to support from more established agencies. There are also at least 79 (22 per cent) districts in England which have no council of voluntary service or equivalent local development agency (LDA). The people managing organisations in these areas are, therefore, likely to be in particular need of advice and support.

Community organisations and village halls

There are around 8,000 village halls in England, managed by perhaps 60,000 or 70,000 trustees under a village hall charitable trust deed. There are perhaps 5,000 multi-purpose community organisations, often constituted as community associations, many of which manage a community centre. There may well be 75,000 to 100,000 trustees involved in their management. The vast majority will be charities – though not necessarily registered.

In addition there are a number of features common to many of these organisations, and particularly those that are charitable. Their Committees and trustees are usually ordinary people elected, not selected, appointed or recruited (although a certain amount of arm-twisting does go on!). Often trustees are elected by the members of an affiliated group to represent them on the governing Committee. This means that trustees often are very committed to the organisation, or part of it.

They may be prepared to commit enormous amounts of time and effort, they may be representative of and accountable to the local community, but they may not have particular management skills. Also, they may or may not have the 'discernment, judgement and strategic vision' that some of those giving evidence have seen as important.

EMPLOYING STAFF

The trustees of organisations which employ paid staff will look to their staff for much of their advice and support. The presence of staff, paid or unpaid, may bring with it other management duties, but it does also provide the opportunity for helping trustees in a number of ways. For example, staff should be able to provide trustees with helpful background information and arrange a suitable induction into the organisation and the Committee. Staff can also make trustees get advice on their legal responsibilities and ensure they are well briefed in issues requiring decision.

Of course, the reality is that these tasks are often not carried out effectively, which then places the trustees in a double difficulty – being poorly served by their staff and still having to manage the same staff who are not doing their job properly.

Role of trustees and staff

Staff also provide trustees with one of their major management responsibilities. Where does the role of the trustees stop and the role of the staff start? What are the responsibilities of the chair as opposed to the senior staff member? These issues are a source of considerable tension and failure to sort them out is one of the major causes of breakdowns in effective management and governance. Problems can often be aggravated by the strong commitment which many trustees have to the organisation, especially those involved in funding it or those with a personal involvement in the cause. Clarifying the respective roles and relationships of the trustees and staff – both the paid and sometimes the voluntary staff – is one of the most important tasks in any voluntary organisation.

PACT

PACT is one of the largest voluntary organisations in Sussex with projects about homelessness, mental health, the environment and young people, as well as community centres and work with elderly people. Eighteen months ago the board decided to take a critical look at the effectiveness of the organisation and, in particular, the financial arrangements with its projects. One of the key results of this review was the simplification of the board structure and the lines of accountability throughout PACT.

The newly established board of directors then began, with their new general manager, to conduct a thorough review of their aims and objectives, the staff work areas, and to develop a way of devising a three-year corporate plan. 'With the help of a facilitator', explains the manager,

> the board were put in a 'gloves-off' situation outside the normal board meeting. They began to see each other and the senior staff team in a new light which has helped them to perform better. Board members have taken on their full responsibility, engaging in all aspects of the organisation: legal, financial and human.

Perhaps the greatest improvement has been the more clearly delineated lines of responsibility between the board and the staff. The board members have also systematically become involved in other distinct pieces of work outside the normal board meetings, such as special events and promotion. The range of discussion and informed debate has greatly improved.

Through the experience of the several informal review and planning sessions, the board members have now developed a trust and understanding of each other and that has helped them to function better in their formal roles. The process enabled the board to raise fundamental questions about the work of PACT and has established a willingness for new people to come through and contribute. 'Above all', says the manager, 'there have been tremendous personal gains with new perspectives and a group of people working well together.'

Artshare Gloucestershire

Artshare Gloucestershire is an organisation committed to equal opportunities and improving access to the arts and creative activity for people with disabilities and mental illness and others who suffer social barriers. They are also determined to provide the management committee with a comprehensive and personalised induction, training and support programme to enable their members to be as actively involved in the running and future direction of the group.

The development co-ordinator explains: 'You need to have a vision and then go out and secure the resources. This is what we've done.' The organisation is currently securing independence from its parent body. The Management Working Party which will become the board of trustees has been developing all the formal governing instruments and policies in an innovative way.

> First we had two independent appraisals of the organisation and established a draft plan. We then ensured that users were involved at the planning stage. To support people in this, we obtained money for training in management committee skills in co-operation with a local college in Gloucester and established individual programmes for individual management committee members' needs. Transport costs were paid and other costs for those needing assistance. We set up a 'buddy system' for those needing help in preparing items for the agenda, writing papers and the necessary follow-up after a meeting. All of this was to ensure we were user-led at the beginning. There has been a collective will to try and do things better.

In addition to management committee meetings, which the co-ordinator accepts are not everyone's strong point, there are four open member meetings a year for those members not on the management committee to express their views to the organisation. Not only is there a commitment to train the management committee and staff, but there is also a provision to train the members who may one day become trustees. This she sees as an investment in the future.

They are planning full induction, ongoing management training and special events to assist members and trustees to understand their roles and responsibilities. There is a determination to use simple language in all their briefing documents to make the structures as accessible as possible. 'If things are too formalised', says the co-ordinator, 'you set up barriers.' She is also a great believer in using independent consultants to help map out a strategic plan which the management committee and staff implement with occasional help from outside. 'Consultancies are useful as a challenging, objective exercise so that we don't become too rigid.'

In the absence of paid staff

Many charities and voluntary organisations have no paid staff, and the trustees have to function both as managers and as workers. Good examples of this type of organisation are the local community organisations in membership of the National Federation of Community Organisations (NFCO). NFCO characterises these as follows:

- unincorporated associations of local people;
- charitable organisations with social welfare and leisure/education objects;
- annually elected management committees;
- volunteer managed and operated;
- managing community premises; and
- umbrella/networking organisations with public membership.

NFCO is concerned that people running these organisations are having to cope with more and more demanding management tasks without the resources to give them the support they require.

There are also larger organisations where volunteer staff are used to run the organisation on a day-to-day basis – for example the Girl Guides or the Women's Royal Voluntary Service.

HOW THE COMMITTEE WORKS

The effectiveness of trustees will also be influenced by the way in which the Committee functions. The following factors are all significant:

- the size of the Committee: many Committees with over 30 members are too large to work effectively;
- the composition of the Committee: sometimes Black and ethnic minorities or disabled people can be made to feel very unwelcome not only as a consequence of being in a minority but also because of the way in which the Committee functions;
- the powers of the Committee: the Committee comprises the charity trustees or may delegate its powers to sub-committees;
- the role of the chair: effective chairing of a Committee, including clear leadership, is crucial to success;
- the servicing of the Committee: the quality of the paperwork the Committee receives can also be very important; and
- the Committee procedures: sometimes these are clear and understood – often they are not.

All these variables will affect the ability of an individual

trustee to perform effectively. It may often be more important to improve the ways in which the Committee is functioning than to provide training for its trustees. The difficulty is that it is not always clear who should take the lead in trying to bring about these improvements. Normally it should be the chair, but if the chair is also part of the problem it may have to be other trustees or the senior staff member (where there is one).

The role of the trustees outside the formal Committee meetings is also very important. A good chair will provide support and guidance to senior staff members and leadership to the organisation on a day-to-day basis. Effective governance involves more than just having well-run Committee meetings. All trustees should bring an enquiring mind to the role.

SUMMARY

In this chapter we have:

- emphasised the different challenges involved in managing organisations at different stages of development;
- stressed the importance of involving members of an organisation in the development of structures rather than simply imposing them on the organisation;
- noted the different ways in which national and local networks can provide trustees with advice and support;
- discussed the implications of having paid or unpaid staff;
- noted that the effectiveness of trustees is often influenced by the way in which the Committee functions;
- emphasised the importance of one person, normally the chair, taking responsibility for improving Committee arrangements; and
- recognised that the role of the chair and other trustees is far wider than simply being involved in meetings.

The significance of all these points is that it will often be more important to address issues concerning the organisational, staffing or Committee environment rather than concentrating solely on providing advice, support and training to individual trustees.

3 Obstacles to effectiveness

INTRODUCTION

It is vital to recognise and confront the various reasons why trustees are often ineffective in practice. In this way we can avoid complacency and refute the unfair criticism that there is something inherently ineffective in the structure of charities and voluntary organisations.

Obstacles to effectiveness include:

- lack of public recognition of the work of trustees;
- trustees' unwillingness to manage;
- trustees' dependence on, and the power of, the paid staff of the organisation;
- complexity and professionalism of charities and voluntary organisations; and
- confusion about accountability.

LACK OF RECOGNITION

The social value attached to service on the majority of voluntary committees is generally very low. Individuals have to be highly motivated to keep up a necessary level of commitment. Without such motivation, it is difficult for many organisations to recruit and retain the people they need.

This lack of public recognition should be addressed imaginatively and, although this issue is outside our terms of reference, we put forward a number of suggestions for further consideration in our conclusions in Chapter 20.

There is a sense in which trustees carry unlimited responsibility for their organisation, while the staff's responsibilities are limited and defined by their contracts of employment. This distinction reveals the source of authority and potential for leadership within a voluntary body, but it is one which is not often recognised by either the general public or trustees themselves. Greater recognition would provide trustees with the confidence and motivation to implement their decisions (particularly where these are resisted).

UNWILLINGNESS TO MANAGE

Some trustees, having been recruited by friends or colleagues, are reluctant to offer firm direction to the organisation. They come on to the Committee because they want to be involved, not because they want to manage the organisation.

Often people are recruited because of their position in other organisations. If Committees are filled with representatives of other organisations, and there is lack of clarity whether they are there to represent the interests of another agency or as members in their own right, they are unlikely to offer the leadership that the organisation needs for itself.

Community and user representatives may be unsure whether it is legitimate to question the work of the organisation. This is a consequence of representation rather than real commitment to the principle of user involvement in the management of charities.

Respect for the commitment and hard work of staff can lead to an abrogation of responsibility by trustees. This arises from confusing the wish to be good and appreciative employers with the need to scrutinise the work of staff for the benefit of the charity.

The fear of making mistakes can immobilise a Committee, restricting its attention and energy to uncontroversial issues. In reality, occasional errors are unavoidable and are part of the process of confronting and working through difficulties. It is easy for trustees to see themselves as marginal or transient figures, without any real authority. The fact that management always concerns the direction and development of a changing situation compounds this problem for trustees. Effective organisations are continually evolving and the foresight to address in good time the issues of a changing situation is a vital feature of the trustee's role.

When things go wrong . . .

1 A charity which drew its trustees from a number of related organisations found some of these trustees were unable to recognise that their responsibilities as trustees were in the first place to the charity.

Inevitably there were conflicts of interests with different trustees working towards goals and objectives that fulfilled the aims of their representative organisation rather than the charity.

2 A charity recognised that its trustees were individuals within the service provision field. It was thought appropriate that there should be a person with financial skills, and a businessman was appointed to the board.

After the first year he realised that there was a widening income gap due to reduced income and ever-increasing costs. He felt it necessary to make cuts in service provision to ensure the ongoing future of the charity and to ensure that the directors would not be liable for 'wrongful trading'.

Some of the other trustees thought the charity was being 'hijacked' by the businessman and were concerned that the charity ethos was being eroded.

The businessman found that all his attempts to curtail spending were overruled and, although he was trying to impose financial controls, the charity was foundering.

3 A charity's board included several individuals who were confusing the role of patrons with that of trustees and thought they were merely lending their names. When they did attend trustee meetings they merely rubber-stamped and 'went along' with decisions.

Due to serious funding cutbacks, plans had to be implemented to reduce core services. Time had to be spent in meetings and discussions and the trustees found they did not have the necessary background knowledge about the charity. They were also unable to cope with the increased time and decision-making pressures and elected to leave the board when they were most needed.

One advantage of trustees undergoing training is that, in raising the profile of their role, they will be encouraged to be assertive enough to scrutinise the management of their organisations.

DEPENDENCE ON STAFF

In an organisation of any size with paid staff, the Committee becomes dependent on the staff for information and guidance. It is essential that Committee members have the necessary background information and knowledge of the organisation to make their own judgements.

New members need to prepare themselves carefully, so that they understand the work of the organisation; the induction of trustees is therefore crucial to their effectiveness. Their training should at the least ensure they understand the accounts and their responsibilities as employers.

One of the problems of being a trustee, particularly a new trustee, concerns a sense of 'impostorship'. Organisations are easily dominated by their professional staff: trustees are lay members who find themselves directing such organisations. New trustees also face the established orthodoxy of the Committee they join. This will tend to insist on opinions and pre-established methods. In any organisation, there are intrinsic conflicts – conflicts of ideas, methods and means; and of principle and value-judgements. The effect of these interactions can easily undermine the confidence of trustees, making them unsure of their role or effectiveness within the organisation.

In larger organisations especially, the staff are key to enabling trustees to be more effective. It is important that staff recognise their responsibilities towards their trustees. With increasingly professional management of charities this is a matter of increasing significance. Working with Committees should be part of staff training.

Staff often underestimate how much power they actually have in relation to their trustees – for example through controlling the flow of information to them. Greater awareness of this point is often the first step towards improving working relationships.

If the Committee becomes an endorsing body, leaving staff to decide policies and run the organisation, the charity may go into decline when key staff leave, and the Committee become vulnerable.

A passive Committee may not have the capacity to act decisively to protect the charity in a crisis.

The Charities Effectiveness Review Trust has described how organisations can benefit from consultancy in resolving the confused relations of staff and Committees. For example, to:

- examine working relationships among national officers, chairmen of major charities, national executive and regional officers, and between them and senior members of staff;
- review and recommend a 'code of conduct' for honorary officers and members which will be binding on them and senior members of staff;
- examine the composition of the board and its responsibilities, frequency of meetings, appointment of office holders;
- assist in creating a structure for policy-making and management of the association which will channel the energies of board members and trust directors and provide a realistic mechanism for involving the membership;
- clarify roles and responsibilities of staff and trustees; and
- define the distinctive and separate roles of honorary officers, voluntary members and paid staff.'

Contacts, training and support from outside the organisation are an important resource in maintaining the independent authority and effectiveness of trustees in relation to the organisation.

COMPLEXITY OF THE ORGANISATIONS

Many voluntary organisations require some of the sophisticated management skills – for example in finance, marketing, personnel, strategic planning – of successful businesses. Trustees have to respect professional managers' competence without abdicating their own responsibilities for the overall governance of the organisation.

Some trustees are recruited because of their own professional competence. Others are service users or members of the community. In a 'contract culture', a trend towards a more professionalised staff may also lead to a more professionalised Committee. It is important that organisations consider the balance of different kinds of experience that they need and do not use recruitment as a substitute for training.

There is increasing awareness among trustees – for example in workshops run by the Centre for Voluntary Organisation at the London School of Economics – of issues about the composition and membership of the Committee – including recruitment, loyalty, motivation, attendance, participation, leadership succession, representativeness, conflicting interests, consumer involvement, the staff role, professional input, composition of national governing bodies in membership organisations, and links with funders.

Training and support for trustees has to be linked with the recruitment and induction of people with the skills and experience relevant to the needs of the organisation.

CONFUSION ABOUT ACCOUNTABILITY

The many ways in which a voluntary organisation is thought to be accountable are complex, and claims of accountability – for example to the users of services or a community – are more easily declared than demonstrated.

Some funders are taking more interest in the effective management of the organisations they support, and this interest is to be welcomed, but the distinction between interest and interference has to be maintained.

Trustees therefore have to exercise considerable judgement in determining how they should respond to the interests of all the people with a stake in the organisation. The skills involved in ensuring that the organisation is accountable, while retaining its independence, are as important as financial and other business skills.

The following three examples illustrate the kinds of situation which can arise when trustees fail to discharge their responsibilities.

Examples of inaction

The only paid employee of a national campaigning organisation became concerned about the actions of one trustee and the inaction of the others.

The organisation had fallen dormant but was resurrected with the appointment of the full-time employee and active involvement from supporters and volunteers. The organisation had three high-profile trustees.

One trustee stated that she did not consider herself responsible for the management of the organisation but had a close relationship with the main founder. At the same time, she was unwilling to resign. A second trustee had never played an active role in the organisation. A third trustee had taken a more active role but was now saying that she wanted to disassociate herself from the organisation, although she publicly used her association with the organisation, for example on her letterhead.

In this situation none of the three trustees were prepared to accept their responsibilities.

The management committee of a local short life housing association had all resigned because of the impending bankruptcy of the organisation. The management committee were saying they were not responsible for the financial position of the organisation and that at the AGM they had elected a new person onto the management committee who would take this responsibility. Although the individual was interested and willing to be involved with the organisation, she did not attend the AGM and did not agree to be elected. The staff were reluctant to approach either the local law centre or the citizens' advice bureau, as there were connections with members of the management committee.

The worker in a small charity with an annual income of more than £100,000 was concerned about the lack of accountability. She did not know of a management committee meeting or AGM having taken place within the last year. There were no invitation letters or minutes and no one seemed to know whether the management committee membership list of six was still current. All the staff were geographically isolated, working from home with only the director and an administrator at head office. She was concerned that the organisation and its activities had been presented in a misleading way to funders. As a member of staff, she expected to know who exactly was on the

management committee. She would like to have the right
to see management committee and AGM notices and
minutes.

The training and support of trustees should address
these skills, including the ability to manage differences
of judgement among trustees themselves, or with staff in
the organisation, when the interests of different people
with a stake in the organisation seem to be in conflict.

SUMMARY

In this chapter we have discussed five different obstacles
to the effectiveness of trustees:

- lack of public recognition of the work of trustees;
- trustees' unwillingness to manage;
- trustees' dependence on the paid staff of the organisation;
- complexity and professionalism of voluntary organisations; and
- confusion about accountability.

In Parts Four and Five of our report we suggest ways of
overcoming these obstacles.

4 New challenges

INTRODUCTION

Trusteeship is a difficult role to perform and it is a role which is likely to become even more demanding in future years.

In this chapter we discuss four aspects of the current context for voluntary organisations, which are likely to increase the challenges facing trustees:

- expansion and contraction in the voluntary sector;
- increasing emphasis on the accountability of the sector;
- the emergence of the 'contract culture';
- the development of a legal framework for charities and voluntary organisations.

The successes, but even more the failures of charities and voluntary organisations are coming under scrutiny from increasing media interest.

EXPANSION AND CONTRACTION IN THE VOLUNTARY SECTOR

The voluntary sector has grown not only in terms of numbers of voluntary organisations but also in terms of turnover and funding. There are now around 170,000 registered charities in England and Wales compared with 140,000 in 1981. Four thousand new charities are registered every year and an untold number of other voluntary organisations are formed. The turnover of the voluntary sector is now estimated at £17 billion per annum compared with approximately £10 billion in 1980/81.

As a result of the overall growth in the last decade the number of staff employed in the voluntary sector has increased significantly in recent years and has most recently been estimated at up to 220,000 paid staff. Much of this growth has been among small and medium-sized organisations, who are often taking on responsibilities of employing staff for the first time. The development of more decentralised structures within national networks has also been a contributing factor to this growth. Some parts of the voluntary sector have grown particularly rapidly, often as a direct result of

government policy. For example, government funding of housing associations will have doubled in the space of three years from £1 billion in 1990/91 to £2 billion in 1993/94.

More recently, however, there are signs that some of these funding sources have begun to slow down or even decline in real terms. Competition for resources is therefore increasing and some organisations are having to reduce their operations and even make staff redundant. Funding crises are becoming more commonplace because of local government cutbacks, changes in government funding programmes, such as the change from the Community Programme to Employment Training, and also the impact of the recession on charitable giving. A 1991 survey of local government funding by NCVO revealed a cut in real terms of £30 million between 1990/91 and 1991/92. At the same time voluntary organisations are having to look to alternative forms of income generation as a means of survival.

All these developments are therefore adding to the financial and personnel responsibilities of trustees. Managing expansion and contraction is likely to become an increasingly important part of the work of trustees.

INCREASING ACCOUNTABILITY

The growth in funding of the voluntary sector has been accompanied by an increase in accountability required by funders. Not surprisingly, most funders are no longer content to give general donations without any clear idea of how their money is being spent or what is being achieved. Clearer business plans, performance indicators and more explicit monitoring and evaluation procedures are all being required. Open-ended grants are increasingly being replaced by more tightly specified service agreements or contracts. The recent Scrutiny Review into government funding of the voluntary sector has reinforced many of these trends.

The general public also expects higher standards of accountability. With the level of funds raised through appeals and fundraising campaigns increasing, the scrutiny to which the charities managing these funds are subjected also becomes more intense. The media are likely to be on the lookout for evidence of maladministration, particularly if it can be shown that funds are not reaching their intended beneficiaries.

Accountability to users of services is also being increasingly emphasised. Users are no longer content to be the passive recipients of services designed and developed on their behalf. They want to be involved in the planning and even the management of those services – to ensure they are sensitive and appropriate to their needs. User involvement is therefore becoming an important issue for voluntary organisations to address, whether by formal or informal means.

For those organisations with a 'democratic' philosophy, accountability to their members is another important factor. This is particularly evident when the proposals to increase membership subscriptions are made.

Growing emphasis on accountability – to funders, users and members – presents a particular challenge to trustees, since they are the people who are held to account. Yet our evidence suggests that most funders never come into contact with the trustees of the organisations they fund, and many trustees have little or no contact with users.

THE 'CONTRACT CULTURE'

The shift from grants towards more tightly specified contractual funding agreements is one important dimension of the 'contract culture'. Another equally important trend over the past few years has been the Government's emphasis on contracting out public services to the private and voluntary sectors. Both local authorities and health authorities have been encouraged to develop their 'enabling' role through concentrating on the purchase rather than the provision of service.

One example of this trend is the NHS and Community Care Act 1990 which requires local authorities to develop a pluralistic pattern of provision through developing the role of the 'independent' sector in community care. Similar developments have been encouraged in housing, through expanding the role of housing associations in housing provision, and in employment training. The recent White Papers and Bills on the future of local government and the Citizen's Charter give continued emphasis to the theme of contracting out.

These developments have important implications for many voluntary organisations. Clearly their responsibilities will be greatly increased, as is evident from the dramatic growth of the housing association movement in the last few years. In some cases they will be taking over responsibility for local authority staff and facilities; in other cases they will be developing new provision under contract to the purchasing authority. As these voluntary organisations' budgets and staffing increase, so do the liabilities of their trustees. Furthermore these liabilities are far more explicitly stated than hitherto as 'contracts' increasingly become the norm.

In many cases new voluntary organisations may be formed to manage these services. For example, a number of trusts have been formed to manage local authority residential homes – thus taking advantage of the financial benefits available until recently from social security payments. Similarly, tenants groups are being encouraged to take over the management of their own housing. Trusts are also being formed by local authorities to run leisure facilities, such as sports centres and museums. These arrangements are seen as opening up access to charitable funding sources as well as other financial benefits such as the mandatory rate relief to which charities are entitled. In these situations, trustees are, overnight, taking on responsibilities involving millions of pounds. Local management of schools also involves similar responsibilities.

There are wider implications of these developments for the voluntary sector as a whole, with questions about how far the independence of the voluntary sector could become compromised as it becomes a major provider of services under contract to government. Will such voluntary organisations be able to maintain their innovative campaigning role as their involvement in social provision increases? Will they be able to develop genuine partnerships with government based on joint assessment of need or will they be mere agents working to an agenda set by the purchasers?

Voluntary organisations are going to need advice and support in order to take on these new responsibilities. Legal advice will be particularly important, but so will advice on strategic planning, negotiation, financial management and many other aspects of running a business. Charities will be seen more as not for profit businesses, facing the same challenges as firms in the private sector, but with the added difficulty of trying to pursue more complex, social objectives rather than simply trying to ensure a profit.

The challenges facing trustees in this new culture are considerable. Their liabilities will be increased, yet their actual involvement in managing their organisations could decrease. Professional staff will be taking the lead role in contract negotiations and contract management, and there will be a danger that trustees are simply left to rubber-stamp their decisions. Meanwhile, fundamental questions such as the future role and direction of the organisation, the involvement of users and the costs and benefits of becoming immersed in providing services in the contract culture may go undebated. Establishing the role of the trustees in these new circumstances and ensuring that they are well equipped to address these questions is therefore going to be particularly important.

THE LEGAL FRAMEWORK

Many of the developments discussed above are also reflected in the way in which the legal framework for voluntary organisations is developing. The Charities Act 1992 was a response to the growth of the voluntary sector and the need for increased accountability. New requirements for charity accounts, increased controls on fundraising methods and strengthened powers for the Charity Commission are all part of a general move to modernise the framework within which charities operate and thus raise standards and increase public confidence. Already, the capacity of the Charity Commission to monitor and regulate the affairs of charities has been greatly strengthened.

At the same time, other aspects of the legal framework within which the voluntary sector has to operate are constantly changing. For example, changes in company law and in local government legislation have both had important implications for many voluntary organisations. Likewise, the introduction of the single market in Europe and the moves towards harmonisation of regulations such as those on VAT and competition will all affect voluntary organisations. There has also been a general tightening up by government bodies such as the Inland Revenue and Customs and Excise, and a number of regulations and licensing requirements, for example, on buildings and sale of goods have been extended and strengthened.

As a result, many charity trustees are often uncertain as to whether or not they are acting within the law. Others, perhaps the majority, are not even aware that they may be acting illegally. A few examples illustrate the complexity of the legal framework for charities:

- Both the Charity Commission's guidance and the Local Government Acts' prohibitions on political activity leave many charities and voluntary organisations in a grey area, where trustees need to act with circumspection, and if necessary seek advice from the Charity Commission.
- The proposals for controlling fundraisers and public collections in the Charities Act 1992, though welcome in their objectives, are extremely complex

and will be very difficult for most voluntary organisations to understand and implement.

- The responsibilities of trustees regarding charity investments are likewise very complex. The Charity Commission has recently reminded charities about them in the wake of the BCCI case, but it is still unlikely that many trustees fully understand their responsibilities in this area.
- Increasing emphasis on trading and contracting raises the issues of what is and is not charitable trading, what kind of organisational forms are most appropriate for these activities and what the financial relationships should be between charities and their trading arms.

Trustees who fail in their responsibilities may be held personally liable for any losses incurred by the charity. Nor does incorporation necessarily protect trustees from personal liability. In view of this, there is considerable interest in the Charity Commission's recent ruling that charitable funds can now be used to insure trustees against liability. This is already common practice in the US and is now likely to become so here. Similarly, there is considerable interest in the idea of developing a new form of legal personality for charitable trusts instead of having to rely on company law.

Though very welcome, none of these developments on insurance and limited liability reduce the need for advice, support and training for trustees in order to cope with situations when questions of personal liability arise. Trustees must therefore be aware of how the legal framework is developing, as well as making sure that their organisations maintain the highest standards possible.

SUMMARY

In this chapter we have highlighted four features of the current environment for voluntary organisations which are likely to add to the difficulties trustees already have in doing their job effectively:

- expansion and contraction in the voluntary sector;
- increasing emphasis on the accountability of the sector;
- the emergence of the 'contract culture'; and
- the development of the legal framework for voluntary organisations.

These challenges all add to the need for increased advice, support and training for trustees discussed in Chapter 5.

5 The need for advice, support and training

INTRODUCTION

Trustees and Committees are central concepts in the charitable and voluntary sectors in England. They are not only legally responsible for the affairs of their organisations; their unpaid, 'voluntary' status is also one of the defining characteristics of the voluntary sector. Without them, there would, literally, be no voluntary sector.

The way in which trustees exercise their responsibilities has significant implications for charities and other voluntary organisations. An effective Committee will have a positive impact on the organisation. An ineffective Committee is unlikely to be able to steer an organisation out of difficulties or help it to meet new challenges it may be facing. Where there are no paid staff, an ineffective Committee will inevitably mean an ineffective organisation.

Equally, from the point of view of individual trustees, those who are fully aware of their duties and liabilities and who have the skills and experience to carry them out effectively are much more likely to avoid any personal difficulties arising from their trusteeship than those who do not.

Trustees need a range of qualities and abilities, both individually and collectively within their Committees, if they are to do their job properly. It is also important for the well-being of the voluntary sector as a whole that they have these qualities and abilities.

In this chapter we argue three propositions:

- first, there is considerable evidence to suggest that many trustees do *not* do their job as effectively as they should;
- second, the 'solution' to the 'problem' of ineffective charity trustees involves improving the capacity of those in this role and is not simply a matter of improved recruitment procedures; and
- third, efforts made so far to provide trustees with advice, support and training have had only limited success.

We should emphasise at the outset that the difficulties experienced by trustees are entirely understandable. Charity trustees of other voluntary organisations between them are responsible for a £17 billion a year operation (see p. 7). They have to walk a delicate tightrope between the interests of their users, their members, their funders, their volunteers and their staff. Unlike managers in the commercial world, they do not have the simple, but decisive discipline of the bottom-line. And at present they receive very little advice or support to help them in carrying out these tasks.

A recent report by the National Federation of Community Organisations entitled *Goalposts moving for voluntary organisations – urgency of voluntary management training* commented:

> Voluntary work is the infrastructure of the welfare state. Great Britain can boast the most active and successful voluntary sector. If this paper seems to indicate massive maladministration of the voluntary sector it must be plainly stated that the voluntary sector does not purposefully maladministrate – quite the contrary – volunteers are very moral and responsible people wishing to do things right.
>
> What in fact we see is the total lack of attention to supervision, to standards of advice and information, a massive absence of direction and resources to help in the management training of voluntary organisations. Legislation and agencies have 'shifted the goalposts'. It is not scaremongering to say that if we don't take this subject seriously, the consequences will be for many that the 'game is over'.
>
> It is no longer a question of 'where can we find resources for management training'. The imperative is we know what will happen if the resources are not made available.

Furthermore the environment in which they have to function – both the organisation itself and the wider context of a changing society – usually add to the difficulties they face. It is perhaps significant that Peter Drucker, the leading writer on management in the United States, has turned his attention away from the comparatively straightforward business sector towards the more complex territory of the voluntary sector.

It is also instructive to remember that most managers in the private and public sectors also experience consider able difficulties in doing their job effectively. For example non-executive directors in the private sector have recently been criticised for exercising insufficient control over their chief executives. If management is difficult, voluntary management is particularly difficult. Hence the importance of trying to identify ways of helping those who have taken on the task in voluntary organisations.

Finally, we should remember that many trustees *do* perform their job effectively. To quote Peter Drucker, writing in *What Business Can Learn from Non-profits, Harvard Business Review* July–August 1989):

> The Girl Scouts, the Red Cross, the pastoral Churches – 'our nonprofit organisations – are becoming America's management leaders. In two areas, strategy and the effectiveness of the board, they are practising what most American business only preach.'

The same is true of many voluntary organisations in this country. Our aim is to make it true of *all* voluntary organisations.

CURRENT PERFORMANCE OF TRUSTEES

Evidence regarding the current performance of trustees is drawn from two main sources. First, there are reports from consultants, trainers and others in regular contact with charities and voluntary organisations suggesting that many trustees do not do their job properly. From time to time, crises in voluntary organisations – such as the War on Want case – attract media attention and contribute to a growing public impression that some charities are poorly managed.

Secondly, there is some survey evidence to show that trustees themselves recognise they are not doing their job properly and would welcome additional support. We discuss each of these below.

Survey evidence

Recent studies of the management of voluntary organisations have tended to focus on the role of paid staff or else have not clearly distinguished between the role of trustees and the role of paid staff. Two partial exceptions to this were the URBED report *Managing Urban Change* on the management training needs of urban programme project managers (DOE, 1988) and the report of the St George's House National Training Initiative on *Training for Community Enterprises* (Action Resource Centre, 1989).

The URBED report highlighted the lack of Committee support for project managers and recommended that Committee members receive training, particularly in the recruitment and management of staff. The importance of providing this training was emphasised by the fact that URBED's survey identified 'insufficient training or support' for project managers as the most important underlying cause of management problems.

The St George's House report, which was based on a postal questionnaire sent to 200 Committee members and project managers and on interviews with a range of different community enterprises, highlighted similar needs. The report concluded that 'Committees have a need for skills in exercising their responsibilities, particularly in holding the project manager and staff to account (including, if necessary, dismissing staff), and in running meetings'.

Other sources

Other, more ad hoc surveys confirm this general picture. A survey of lawyers involved in Committees through the Action Resource Centre's 'Lawyers in the Community' scheme shows that even professionals on Committees admit to important gaps in their knowledge which reduce their effectiveness as trustees. Areas identified included employment law, charity law and local government legislation. Similar gaps were identified in a Housing Corporation survey of housing association committees (which tend to comprise many professional people). A need for more knowledge of finance, in particular capital finance and negotiation procedures, was highlighted.

A series of seminars for trustees involving the Charity Commission in Lincolnshire, Nottingham, Suffolk, Wiltshire and Worcester revealed that a majority of those attending had neither read nor actually knew of the existence of their charity's written constitution, thus making it impossible for them to administer their charity properly. A survey of trustees of local charities carried out by Derbyshire Rural Community Council found similar results.

It is significant that virtually all of those submitting evidence to the Working Party argued that many trustees do not do their job properly. They often differed in their views about how best to tackle this problem, but they all agreed that something needed to be done about it.

Specific problems

Examples of the kind of problems experienced by trustees included:

- lack of knowledge and clarity about their role, duties and responsibilities;
- lack of knowledge about their organisation, including its overall mission, its constitution and its governing instrument;
- overload of some trustees, underuse of others;
- conflict between trustees and paid staff; and between chair and senior staff member;
- all the power held by the paid staff;
- concentration on regulation rather than strategic management;
- badly run meetings; and
- unclear or non–existent procedures.

There is evidence that many people are not even aware that they are trustees. They are not referred to as 'trustees' by their organisations and they have not been told about their responsibilities as trustees. This is particularly true of local endowed charities and other local community organisations.

These problems might result in poor performance for the organisation in relation to

- strategic planning;
- financial management;
- property management;
- personnel management;
- guidance to the senior staff member;
- contractual obligations;
- fundraising;
- campaigning;
- accountability; and
- teamwork.

This in turn could result in failure to achieve objectives, loss of funds and even illegal activity.

For the individual trustee these problems might mean

- personal liability;
- conflict;
- stress;
- waste of time;
- disillusionment;

and ultimately resignation or debarment. Over time they are likely to mean it will be increasingly difficult to retain or recruit trustees.

A problem of identification

It seems likely that in hundreds, if not thousands, of cases Committees may not know their organisation is a charity, nor that they are trustees with responsibilities in law. Many organisations have adopted a charitable constitution, such as the National Federation of Community Organisations' model constitution for a community association, without realising that that makes them a charity with a requirement to apply for registration.

Our own survey seems to confirm all these points. Only one in three of our respondents knew that he or she was a trustee. When asked about training and support needs, about a third of respondents felt that more training and support were urgently needed. The main issues identified as blocks or barriers to the effective working of their Committees were relationships with staff (32 per cent), poor decision-making (29 per cent) and lack of clarity regarding the role and purpose of the Committee (24 per cent).

All this evidence points to the conclusion that trustees are experiencing considerable difficulties in carrying out their role effectively. Furthermore the difficulties facing trustees are likely to increase further over the coming years, as we discuss in the next section.

THE ISSUE OF RECRUITMENT

One response to the difficulties faced by trustees is to argue that charities and voluntary organisations should ensure that they recruit trustees who already have all the skills and experience necessary to be an effective trustee.

This argument has to be rejected for both philosophical and practical reasons. First, it undermines the whole ethos of the voluntary sector – the notion of people taking action on their initiative and of their own free will. Many trustees are elected to their position. Commitment and enthusiasm are the most important qualifications for being a trustee. If they also had to have particular skills or experience as a required qualification, then the number of potential trustees would be drastically reduced and the community involvement and public participation would be undermined. The capacity of the voluntary sector to involve a wide range of people and to ensure the representation of different points of view and sections of the community would be drastically reduced. Similarly, the role of the voluntary sector in helping people develop their own capacities and their own self-confidence would be completely lost.

More practically, it is improbable that there would be sufficient people available with the knowledge and experience potentially required of a trustee. We have already noted that a group of professional lawyers identified a number of important gaps in their own knowledge – yet presumably they are among the more experienced and qualified members of society in this field. Furthermore, trustees will need to acquire new areas of knowledge as the legal and policy context for their organisation's activities changes and develops.

A more fundamental objection to this response is that being an effective trustee is not simply a matter of having a particular type of business experience or acquiring a particular body of knowledge. Indeed, it is significant that people who may be highly successful in one setting, for example on the board of a private company or as a member of a local authority, are often very unsuccessful on the Committee of a voluntary organisation. This is not to argue that experience in other sectors may not sometimes be very useful, but simply to emphasise that running a voluntary organisation is not the same as running a private company or a local authority.

The extent of the 'uniqueness' of the demands of management in the voluntary sector is very much a subject for debate. Voluntary organisations need to know about market research, business planning, marketing and about performance review as much as any private company. However, the multiple objectives pursued by voluntary organisations, their emphasis on user involvement and empowerment, their interest in campaigning as well as service provision, their voluntary ethic, their concern with people's special needs and their uncertain finances – and, of course, their unpaid trustees – all combine to present a particular management challenge. None of these characteristics is unique to the voluntary sector, but taken together they present a different task for those who have to govern them.

Some of the skills needed to manage in the voluntary sector may be taught, some may be developed through experience, others will be learned on the job. However, it could still be argued that provided these skills can be specified, then the best approach to improving voluntary sector management is to recruit trustees who meet this specification, as one might recruit staff for a specific post. Yet, the reality is that it would prove to be virtually impossible to draw up a comprehensive specification and then find sufficient people who satisfied it. There will always be a need to help develop the range of skills and knowledge required.

We therefore reject the argument that increasing the effectiveness of trustees is simply a matter of improving recruitment procedures. That is not to deny the importance of specifying the kind of person a trustee needs to be and identifying the range of skills required nor to play down the importance of developing clear job descriptions for trustees. However, in themselves, these approaches will not meet the needs identified earlier. Continued advice, support and training will also be required, both for existing and potential future trustees.

WHAT TRAINING IS AVAILABLE?

Most voluntary sector training is targeted at paid staff rather than trustees. For example, out of the 135 courses in NCVO's 1991/92 short course programme, only seven were directly aimed at Committees. As a result, existing provision is rarely sensitive to the needs of trustees.

The URBED study found that provision needed to be relevant, timely, sensible and acceptable. This was reinforced by the St George's House report which concluded that training for community enterprises needed to be local, accessible, small-scale and informal. Yet the reality is that most provision appears to be inaccessible, inappropriate, unaccepted or non-existent.

Inaccessible

Most existing advice and training is either in the form of leaflets and guidance notes or short courses. The former tend to be written in an inaccessible and legalistic style and as a result are seldom read or understood. More fundamentally, most written material never reaches trustees in the first place because there is no system for ensuring that it does. Less than one trustee in ten in our survey recalled seeing leaflets from the Charity Commissioners, even though a copy of each leaflet is now sent to the correspondents of all charities. Furthermore, insufficient attention has been paid to special needs regarding written material, for example for people who cannot read or speak English.

Short courses are often held during the daytime. They can therefore be very difficult for trustees to get to, quite apart from any considerations of cost. The St George's House report found that some of the main barriers to training for Committees were lack of childcare provision, other commitments, lack of time and lack of motivation. Generally, there is evidence of poor take-up of training courses by Committee members.

Inappropriate

Short courses are not only often inaccessible for trustees, but also inappropriate, because they tend to focus on specific skills rather than relating to the range of issues confronting trustees. It can therefore often be difficult for trustees to apply what they learn to their own particular role and organisation. Advice and support relating to their current experience as a trustee would be a more helpful starting point.

Similarly, one set of written material is unlikely to meet the needs of every kind of trustee. What is needed is a variety of different types of material for different types of organisation at different stages of development. Currently, this variety does not exist.

Distance learning methods also have their shortcomings for trustees. The St George's House report concluded that these methods required too much self-discipline for most trustees' purposes. They will certainly be appropriate for people prepared to devote a considerable amount of time to training, but these are likely to be in the minority.

More generally, existing provision tends to be one-off and unrelated to the experience of trustees, rather than ongoing and relevant.

Resistance

Many trustees are resistant to the notion of 'training'. Having volunteered to take on the role, they are unwilling to spend large amounts of time undergoing training and, in many cases, do not feel they need training. Just under half the trustees in our survey felt that, while training was 'a good thing', there were no obvious or immediate needs relating to their own organisations. A substantial number felt that training was probably appropriate for some of the other trustees, but, by implication, not for themselves. And yet, it is clear that most trustees would greatly benefit from a range of different types of advice and support.

A fundamental difficulty is that currently it is very unclear where the responsibility lies for ensuring this advice and support is provided. Unless its importance is recognised, it will be difficult to make progress. At present, it is often those who most need support who are most resistant to it. Fear of the unknown can also be another factor. We need to find ways of presenting the whole concept of training in more acceptable ways, so that it becomes the norm for trustees, in the same way as it is for magistrates and school governors.

Non-existent

Finally, there are many forms of advice and support which simply do not exist. For example, there is no general recognised handbook for use by trustees and there are no videos for use in training sessions with trustees. There is also a shortage of specialist, low-cost advisers on some of the legal and other technical issues facing trustees. Even many of the high-cost advisers are not necessarily experienced in all aspects of charity law. Induction and briefing arrangements for trustees appear particularly weak. Our own survey found just over one trustee in five had been through a recognisable induction process. Roughly the same number again spoke of receiving an informal briefing. Improved induction arrangements would be widely supported.

A further concern is that some existing sources of advice are disappearing. For example, law centres, councils for voluntary service and citizens advice bureaux have all suffered significant cutbacks in local authority funding. Also, some local authority sources of advice, such as county councils' legal departments, are now under a double threat of local government re-organisation and being contracted out.

Generally, there is a serious lack of suitable provision of advice, support and training for trustees. Nor has there been any attempt in recent years to assess what is needed or any national initiative to improve on current provision.

SUMMARY

In this chapter we have argued that:

- there is considerable evidence to suggest that many trustees do not do their job effectively.
- the solution to these difficulties is not simply a matter of improved recruitment procedures.
- if we are to encourage the participation of people from all walks of life in the running of our voluntary organisations, then we must ensure that the right kind of advice, support and training is available for trustees.
- too much current provision is inaccessible, inappropriate and unwanted. Many forms of advice and support just do not exist.

There is therefore a clear need to develop new forms of advice, support and training for trustees.

PART TWO
Roles and responsibilities of trustees

6 Legal responsibilities of trustees

Introduction

We are aware that many trustees do not understand the nature of their legal responsibilities, or, if they are aware, do not know how to carry them out. It is essential that trustees know that they are trustees and what their responsibilities are. Many Committee members have an incomplete awareness of what their organisation can and cannot do as a charity.

The governing instrument should say how trustees are appointed. The people responsible for the general control and management of the administration of the charity are defined as charity trustees by the Charities Act 1960, but they will not necessarily be called trustees in the governing instrument of the charity: council of management, executive committee, management committee, board of governors or board of directors are common alternatives. Even though these charity trustees may delegate some of their powers to other committees or officers of the charity, they are the individuals who ultimately control the administration of the charity and therefore bear the legal responsibilities, and if the charity suffers loss as a consequence they may be held personally liable to make good the loss to the charity.

Charity trustees are sometimes confused into thinking that they are not the 'real' trustees because of a second category of holding or custodian trustees. As indicated in Chapter 1, holding trustees have the limited function of holding the assets of the charity (and all investments) for safe keeping.

Trustees are responsible for ensuring that the charity is abiding by its objects and constitution.

PERSONAL LIABILITY

Trustees should be aware of their responsibility, as outlined in the Charity Commission leaflet CC3. While many are unaware of their responsibilities, some trustees have become concerned about their personal liability as trustees. In practice most trustees, bearing in mind their responsibilities and overseeing the work of a charity with prudent financial planning, have little need for concern about their personal liability.

Nevertheless trustees are personally liable not only for misapplication of funds but also for losses caused to the charity by their failure to exercise due standards of care or by acts which are outside their powers (for example, purchasing investments which are not authorised investments under the charity's governing instrument). The courts, however, have power to relieve trustees from liability where they have acted both honestly and reasonably.

Once an individual accepts the office of trustee, he or she becomes jointly liable for the administration of the charity. A trustee cannot escape responsibility either by remaining inactive, leaving the other trustees to make decisions, or by delegating the administration to other individuals or committees (unless expressly authorised to do so under the governing instrument of the charity). A trustee, for example, will not escape a liability for financial shortcomings on the grounds that the finances of the charity were a matter delegated to the treasurer or finance committee of which the trustee in question was not a member.

The personal responsibility of trustees does not prevent their employing staff or agents to implement their decisions. They have a statutory power to do so. They will not be personally liable for the wrongful acts of employees or agents, provided they exercise proper care in making the appointment and in supervising the appointee.

Similarly, trustees may delegate their decision-making powers to sub-committees (whether consisting of trustees or non-trustees) provided this is expressly permitted by the governing instrument of the charity. Statutory powers of delegation are severely restricted and there is no implied power of delegation. Where trustees have power to delegate, they will not be liable for the faults of those to whom they have delegated discretionary powers, provided they monitor the sub-committee in question. Otherwise they may be liable for losses suffered by the charity as a result of their own lack of care and diligence.

The training of trustees has a most important contribution to make in raising understanding among trustees about these legal responsibilities and liability, in a way that does not discourage them from taking up the responsibilities in a positive way.

DIFFERENT TYPES OF LIABILITY

When considering the liability of trustees it is essential that the different types of liability are distinguished.

Liability for breach of trust

All charity trustees, whether of an incorporated or unincorporated charity, are potentially personally liable for breach of trust. This liability can arise if they have failed in their duty of care, that is to act as reasonable and prudent businessmen and women and the charity has suffered financial loss as a result. It can also arise if they do not have proper regard to the purposes of the charity or act where they do not have power.

This could occur, for example, if, without taking appropriate professional advice, they invested in speculative investments with resulting loss to the charity. Trustees can also be personally liable for breach of trust if they act outside the charity's objects or powers or in breach of charity law. This can occur if they engage in unpermitted political activities, in which case they could be personally liable to repay the charity funds spent on the unauthorised activities. They would also be personally liable if they granted loans to an associated trading company at less than the full commercial rate of interest.

Where there is a breach of trust it is normally up to the Attorney General to decide whether he will require the charity trustees to repay any loss to the charity or reimburse any unauthorised expenditure. Ultimately an action against the trustees could be pursued through the courts. In practice trustees have only rarely repaid any loss or reimbursed expenses.

Liability to third parties in contract and tort

Contractual liability arises where a charity enters into a contract, for example for the supply of goods or services. Liability for tort is liability for such action as trespass, nuisance or breach of statutory duty. In the case of an incorporated charity, the charity itself enters into contracts, holds property, and sues and is sued in its name, so an individual charity trustee would be protected from personal liability in such cases in the first instance. If the contract constituted a breach of trust, however, the trustee could be ultimately personally liable. If the charity is not incorporated trustees will be

personally liable, though they may be able to claim against the charity's funds if they have not committed a breach of trust.

Liability under the Insolvency Act 1986

Under this Act directors of a charitable company (who are in effect 'charity trustees') can be personally liable to repay sums to an insolvent company where they have been guilty of wrongful trading, that is to say they have continued to operate when they knew or ought to have known that liabilities could not be met from liquid assets.

The Insolvency Act 1986 has been applied to industrial and provident societies, and S.220 of the Act defines unregistered companies to include 'any association', so it appears that this could be applied to any incorporated body.

Vicarious liability

A point that is sometimes overlooked is that charity trustees will remain liable where an employee fails to carry out his or her duties, and may be vicariously liable for the actions of their employees in the course of their employment.

CARE AND DILIGENCE

In carrying out their responsibilities, trustees must act with the same diligence and care as men and women 'of ordinary prudence and vigilance would in the management of their own affairs'. This has been interpreted to mean that they should act as ordinary prudent men and women of business. (If trustees receive remuneration, which does happen in exceptional circumstances, a higher standard of diligence is expected.)

This duty to act with diligence and care requires action from the trustees, for example to satisfy themselves about the probity of staff and the accuracy of financial records. Absence of bad faith or dishonesty will not protect a trustee from liability for losses suffered by the charity as a consequence of the trustee's inactivity. Ignorance of facts will not necessarily protect a trustee from liability. Whether or not a trustee has acted reasonably is judged according to the facts which he or she knew or ought to have known.

The duty to act as prudent men and women of business assumes an awareness of financial and legal issues, although not a detailed and technical knowledge.

Trustees should know when it is advisable to seek and consider professional advice, without having a detailed knowledge of the subject matter of the advice. They need to be aware of their responsibilities as employers of staff, owners of premises and investors of funds, but without having a detailed knowledge of employment law, contract, property law and financial markets. To have taken and followed professional advice will not necessarily protect trustees from a claim that they have failed in their duties, but it will be evidence of their having acted with care and diligence if they behaved reasonably in acting on the advice.

These responsibilities are not well understood by the majority of trustees, and the need for specialist support and advice is self-evident. In many cases the trustees will rely on the particular expertise of individuals. It is very important that trustees with specialist knowledge and experience communicate this knowledge to fellow trustees, as all are in the end accountable for any actions taken on behalf of the charity.

LIMITING LIABILITY

It is generally understood that trustees of an unincorporated charity – a trust or an association – may be personally liable for losses suffered by the charity and the debts of the charity. However, there is a common misconception that trustees of an incorporated charity are protected from personal liability. This is only partially correct.

The responsibilities described in this chapter apply to all charity trustees, whatever the form of the charity. If a trustee fails in these responsibilities and the charity suffers loss as a result, the trustee may be held personally liable to make good the loss, whether the charity is incorporated or unincorporated.

The Charity Commission has recently ruled that charitable funds may be used to take out insurance policies to protect trustees in certain circumstances. This is now very common practice in the US. However, although this is a welcome development, it in no way reduces the need for trustees to be fully aware of their legal responsibilities.

SUMMARY

In this chapter we have examined the legal responsibilities of trustees and discussed the different ways in which they could be personally liable.

It is clearly important that trustees are aware of these responsibilities and are provided with the advice, support and training to enable them to discharge them effectively.

7 Financial responsibilities of trustees

INTRODUCTION

Trustees are responsible for the good administration of the finance of the organisation, and have to understand that they may be held accountable for any misuse of funds.

They therefore have responsibilities in relation to budgets, accounts, assets and investments, as well as in relation to fundraising, trading and charges.

MANAGEMENT INFORMATION

Decisions are taken by trustees and senior staff members whose time is precious. Consequently, the importance of sound, effective management information systems can not be over-stressed. The days have passed when the necessary information could be recorded without thought. Effective decision making requires effective information. Vital non-financial information should be integrated with financial data to provide effective management information.

In the process of requiring practical, user-friendly information systems trustees should consider:

- exactly what management information is required;
- who needs it and why;
- how it will be prepared and by whom;
- whether it can be obtained as a by-product of another process;
- whether the cost of having the information is commensurate with the benefit;
- if the needs of different users can be catered for by tailoring different reports; and
- for how long information should be stored and when historic information should be deleted or archived.

BUDGETS

Budgets and accounts are not just for information, but are the main instrument for direction and control. Trustees should discuss the organisation's annual budget in terms of planned income and expenditure.

The budget should be formally approved by the trustees and regular reports made to the trustees on actual income and expenditure compared with the budget estimates.

Significant variations should be highlighted for discussion and any major changes to the budget should be agreed by the trustees.

Budgeting and planning and the correct allocation of income and expenditure are of crucial importance to charities, especially where it is necessary to match variable income against fixed commitments. The budgetary control process is required to match short-term activities against longer-term strategy. Good budgeting is required to co-ordinate operations, control subsequent expenditure and provide a means to motivate through targets.

ACCOUNTS

A new trustee should see past accounts, reports and minutes of the trustees' meetings so that he or she can be satisfied that the affairs of the charity have been carried on in accordance with its governing instrument, that the activities are within the objects of the charity and that the proper decision-making processes have been followed. If there have been breaches of trust in the past, a new trustee is not liable for those breaches, but he or she is responsible for preventing continuing breaches and for initiating whatever steps may be possible to recover assets which have been lost in the past.

Trustees should not pretend that administration costs nothing.

Section 32 of the Charities Act 1960 requires charity trustees to prepare accounts for periods not exceeding 15 months. The Charities Act 1992 strengthens the requirements and trustees have a duty to ensure that accounting records are kept in respect of the charity which are sufficient to show and explain all the charity's transactions and disclose at any time, with reasonable accuracy, the financial position of the charity.

In particular, the accounting records should contain a record of all sums of money received and expended by the charity and a record of all assets and liabilities.

When a charity's gross income in a financial year does not exceed £25,000, a simplified form of account may be kept.

INTERNAL CONTROLS AND AUDIT

Due to the need for high public accountability and also to fulfil the trustees' duties and responsibilities, a sound system of internal control is required. At the same time, it is necessary to tailor the systems of control to suit the charity environment. Unrealistic control and demands of accountability from volunteers may be counter-productive. Nevertheless, the charity's trustees and donors have a right to expect that the charity's income, expenditure, assets and liabilities are controlled in an efficient and cost-effective manner. Additionally, funders may require audit certificates prior to making grants or as a requisite of having made a grant.

The Charities Act 1992 introduces for the first time a requirement that charities with a gross income or total expenditure of over £100,000 should have a professional audit. Charities under that limit should have their accounts examined by an independent examiner who is reasonably believed by the trustees to have the requisite ability and practical experience to carry out a competent examination of the accounts.

The audit has to be performed within 10 months of the charity's year end. If it is not done, the Commissioners may appoint independent auditors or examiners and the cost of the audit can be recovered from the trustees.

The trustees are responsible for the stewardship of the charity's funds, and one of their objectives should be to produce financial statements that provide useful and honest information to the readers. The auditors should assist the trustees in attaining this objective.

ASSETS

A new trustee should know what assets belong to the charity and who holds those assets. It is good practice for each charity to prepare an audit of its assets for review by new and existing trustees.

It may be necessary to transfer assets into the name of a new trustee jointly with the other trustees or to change the arrangements, operating bank accounts so that the new trustee is a signatory. Alternatively, if assets are vested in holding or custodian trustees, they should be informed of the appointment of the new trustee.

In general charity trustees have a duty to use the income of the charity. They may accumulate it only:

- in accordance with a power to do so given by the governing instrument or subsequent scheme or order of the charity;
- to meet specific expenditure which will occur in future years; or
- to create a fund for specific projects which they intend to carry out.

Endowments and special funds

Trustees must be aware of special categories within the funds of their charity. They should know whether there is permanent endowment, so that only the income may be used without the authority of the Charity Commission. They should know what funds are general funds and can then be applied for the purposes of the charity without restriction and they should know whether there are special funds which can be applied only for particular purposes, for example funds which have been raised as a result of a special appeal.

Property

If a charity owns land or buildings which are used for its charitable purposes, the trustees must ensure that these are properly insured and maintained. They should also review from time to time the suitability of the property for the purposes of the charity.

The Charities Act 1992 makes new provision with respect to restrictions on the disposition of land held by or in trust for a charity. The disposition must be at the best terms that can reasonably be obtained and should be at arm's length. Proper written advice must be obtained and considered. In the case of a mortgage, the loan must be necessary, the terms must be reasonable and the charity must have the ability to repay on those terms.

INVESTMENTS

Trustees have a responsibility to maximise returns on investments, both in terms of income and capital gain, while minimising risk.

In exercising their powers to invest the funds of the charity, trustees must act as prudent men and women of business making investments on behalf of those for whom they are bound to provide.

If the governing instrument of the charity does not contain express powers of investment, the trustees' powers will be governed by the Trustee Investments Act

1961. In such a case trustees will normally be safe if they comply with the provisions of the Act, including the obligations to obtain advice and to consider the need to diversify their investments. Frequently, the governing instrument gives the trustees much wider powers of investment. Even where that is the case, however, trustees must act reasonably and prudently, should avoid any investment which is speculative, and should consider the need for diversification.

The charity trustees must satisfy themselves as to the scope of investments open to the charity and who is authorised to make investment decisions for the charity. There may be power to delegate the day-to-day management of investments to fund managers who should follow the investment policy agreed by the trustees.

Trustees of charities may sometimes take the view that they do not wish to invest in certain types of business. In a few cases, it may be obvious that a certain type of investment would be inappropriate; for example, a charity for the treatment of alcoholism could hardly be expected to invest in a brewery. In general, however, trustees are obliged to invest so as to obtain the maximum benefit for the charity. Investment advisers will usually be able to offer a number of equally attractive suggestions for investment, and in such a case trustees would not normally be acting improperly in taking ethical factors into account in making a choice between them. However, it would be improper for trustees to take ethical objections to a point where they are unable to maintain an adequately balanced portfolio of investments.

Ethical investment policy

In the light of growing concern over ethical investment, it is important for trustees to review their charity's policies and the powers under which they can act. NCVO was encouraged to do just this by its member organisations and has produced guidance in setting up ethical investment policy.

Trustees should ascertain under what powers they can invest (normally the Trustee Investments Act 1961) and any special powers laid down in their governing instrument. Also, they should review what restrictions are specified, how the investments are to be diversified and the suitability of investments to the trust's objects. The policy must be in the best financial interest of the beneficiaries.

Trustees must secure the best return for the monies invested, but also take into account non-financial considerations. These may be investments which run contrary to the charity's aims, for example investment in a tobacco company by a health organisation. The suitability of investments to the objects is more difficult to determine

and must be considered alongside best return, diversification and prudence.

In NCVO's case, it was decided, after considering its objects and taking legal advice, that at the time it was not appropriate to invest in company groups:

- with over 3 per cent of worldwide workforce in South Africa;
- which do not provide enough information to assess accurately the numbers of employees in South African subsidiaries; or
- where over 3 per cent of their total business is derived from tobacco production, processing or packaging.

It is advisable when establishing an investment policy to set up a sub-committee to consider detailed criteria and identify areas of investment which are compatible with and suitable to the objects of the charity. Trustees should seek advice on how to define specific criteria which are practical to adopt in the charity's circumstances. They also need to establish the potential impact of the criteria on the portfolio of investments and discuss these with investments advisers along with considerations of best return. For organisations with small portfolios, investment in various ethical unit trusts may be considered more appropriate.

It is very important regularly to review the performance of investments with professional advisers. The criteria should be reviewed annually in the light of new information and financial performance. And in order to comply with the Financial Services Act 1986, a Management Agreement must be entered into with the charity's investment advisers. This will include a statement of the ethical investment policy as guidance to the advisers.

Training and support on financial management is important for a wide range of charities, who may not have all the necessary expertise on their own Committee. At any sign of things going wrong, legally or financially, it is essential to seek sound professional advice. In a position of accountability, it is proper, if in any doubt, to disclose information.

FUNDRAISING

There is uncertainty about the individual contribution which may be expected of trustees in relation to fundraising. Some trustees see fundraising as having nothing to do with them. However, the relationship with funders has to be nurtured. There are obvious dangers if fundraising is split off from the general policy direction of the charity. This distancing from fundraising is very different from the experience of Board members of not-for-profit organisations in the United States, where they are expected to contribute generously from their own resources as well as to encourage and influence other donors.

The need for training provision in this field will vary, depending upon the size and nature of the charitable organisation. The needs of trustees in medium/small organisations (and in particular organisations maintained solely by voluntary effort) are likely to be far greater and substantially different from those required of trustees in major national fundraising charities. The dilemma continues to exist that trustees who are active in the former type of charitable organisation are probably in greatest need of training support and yet have the most inadequate resources available to pay for it, and even less opportunity to find out about it.

Legal obligations and fundraising

Trustees are under a legal obligation to ensure that all the activities of charities they are associated with are undertaken in accordance with the objects of the organisation in the most efficient and effective way. There are two general requirements upon all trustees in connection with fundraising:

1 Is all the fundraising activity in accordance with the aims, objectives and mission of the charity? For example, charities may respond to a fundraising opportunity, with limitation of use of the funds now available to them, rather than responding to need. This may lead to a deflection of energy and activity away from the original aims and objectives of the organisation. In such a case trustees must be able to make judgements and, where necessary, to intervene to halt this process. This implies active involvement in the overall operation of the organisation and the ability to analyse and make such complex judgements.
2 Not only should the aims of fundraising be in accord with the mission of the organisation, but the operation of that fundraising activity must be undertaken in a legal, efficient, effective and above all appropriate manner. It is the trustees' ultimate duty to ensure that this is the case.

Fundraising in different sized charities

All forms of fundraising involve greater or lesser degrees of risk. Trustees either actively engaged in fundraising activity or managing these activities in medium and small-sized organisations need to have some quite specific information about the likely benefits and risks of different types of fundraising activity and strategy. Poorly led fundraising initiatives in organisations are a more likely source of potential bankruptcy than any other within our sector.

In the larger national voluntary organisations fundraising practice has now reached an enormously complex and sophisticated level. Rather like non-executive board members in privately owned companies, trustees can be expected to manage a general overview of fundraising activity; to comment on major new initiatives requiring substantial budgetary outlay and in generally steering the overall fundraising strategy of the organisation.

Specific fundraising committees

There is anxiety in voluntary organisations of all shapes and sizes where staff and trustees do not have a clear notion of the specific roles and obligations that they bring to fundraising committees.

In the United States the position is often more clearly defined. Trustees are asked to join fundraising committees on the basis that firstly they themselves will commit a considerable sum of money to the organisation and that secondly they will persuade other major donors to do likewise. Targets are then set against each individual, performance monitored and failure to achieve targets automatically results in removal from the committee.

The experience in England is neither as harsh nor as effective. All too often trustees who are invited to join fundraising committees are not aware that the fundraisers believe that in joining the committee the trustee is undertaking personally to provide support and will also solicit support from others.

Many trustees do not feel confident about fundraising at all. They do not see it as their function and believe it to be a nasty, tacky business. Clearly there is still considerable need to produce well articulated arguments to challenge this view within charities with their own trustees.

CHARGES

Another important aspect of income generation for a charity is the setting of charges for services, including membership subscriptions and charges for newsletters and other publications.

Trustees should formally approve a policy on charges which balances the organisation's need for income against the ability of its users and beneficiaries to pay for the services provided. Regular reports on the impact of charges on usage and membership rates should be made to trustees to enable them to keep these charges under review.

TRADING

Trading is an area of increasing activity by charities, and of increasing complexity for trustees. Many charities carry out 'trading' which is in pursuit of their objects and so is not trading in the eyes of the Inland Revenue and H.M. Customs and Excise, while other types of trading attract corporation tax and VAT. We have heard of some instances of the increasing rigour with which the authorities are applying their regulations, and charities cannot expect to be 'let off' on the assumption of good will towards their activities.

Where trustees of a charity are also directors of an associated trading company, they must ensure that the interests of the charity are not subverted by the commercial interests of the trading company. Trustees in this situation must be able to 'wear two hats' and avoid conflicts of interest. They will often need specialist advice to assist them in this.

In their 1988 report the Charity Commissioners, when discussing trading, stated:

> Trustees have a duty to consider the tax effectiveness of the arrangements between them and any associated trading company, and they may be personally liable to account for taxation liabilities which are unnecessarily incurred directly or indirectly as a result of the in-efficient administration of the charity. It makes no difference that the difficulties may arise not from the disqualification of the investment made by the charities but from the disallowance to the associated trading company of corporation tax relief.

Contrary to popular misconception the taxation of charities is a complex area and the Commissioners believe that ensuring the proper handling of this is part of the trustees' responsibility.

SUMMARY

In this chapter we have examined the various financial responsibillities of trustees, including

- budgets;
- accounts;
- assets, including property;
- investments;
- fundraising;
- charges; and
- trading.

Trustees will need some advice, support and training in all these different aspects to ensure they discharge their responsibilities effectively.

8 Management responsibilities of trustees

INTRODUCTION

Trustees are responsible for the character and personality of their agency: is it lively or sleepy? Is it respected in its constituencies so that it attracts resources? In a word, does it show *vitality* as conditions change? This is a quality which resides in individuals, not in systems.

Trustees have a number of important managerial responsibilities including

- the appointment of, and contractual relationships with, the staff;
- ensuring accountability to funders, users and members;
- representing the views of the organisation on issues relating to the interests of the organisation; and
- strategic planning, including the identification of mission, maintenance of values and evaluation of the organisation's activities.

EMPLOYMENT OF STAFF

Many trustees do not have the expertise or knowledge effectively to recruit, appoint, monitor and appraise staff. A particular difficulty is in the area of grievance and disciplinary procedures.

The tendency is to avoid confrontation, to allow a situation to slip until it reaches a critical point. At this stage, a Committee may overreact and suspend or dismiss an employee without having gone through a disciplinary procedure. The amount of time, energy and solicitors' fees involved in unravelling a dispute can weaken an organisation for months or even years.

At no time must fraud be condoned or poor performance allowed to continue. With clear guidance, well-written and approved procedures and trained Committee members, costly disputes can be avoided.

In addition to an understanding of their responsibilities under employment law, trustees may consider ways in which they can be supportive of their staff in carrying out the work of the charity. For example, many charities have inadequate training budgets, and this is partly a consequence of the reluctance of trustees to invest in the people who are doing the work of the charity.

ACCOUNTABILITY

In addition to their formal legal and financial responsibilities, trustees have a role in ensuring accountability to the different people with a stake in the work of the organisation. These stakeholders may include different funders, donors, users of services, partnership organisations.

Some stakeholders are represented on the Committee; many are not. It is not usually appropriate for funders or individual donors to be on the Committee of an organisation, and if they understand the responsibilities which then arise, they may not want to be.

Users of services may make up a significant part of the Committee – 100 per cent in many cases – and the involvement of users in the management of voluntary organisations is a significant characteristic of the voluntary sector. Users of services are rightly concerned about what they see as tokenism and it is important that those 'representing' minority interests are recognised to be active members in their own right of any Committee on which they serve. At the same time, some users may prefer to be consulted rather than being formally involved in the management of the organisation.

Trustees, including those who may be thought to represent particular interests, have to take account of the interests of all stakeholders in the work of the organisation. In this sense their accountability is more wide-ranging than their specific legal responsibilities suggest.

REPRESENTATION

Trustees will often have to speak for the organisation and represent its views. While having both a right and a duty to campaign on behalf of the beneficiaries of the organisation, trustees must also ensure they comply with the legal restrictions on campaigning.

Trustees must also be able to justify their campaigning activities in terms of effectiveness and value for money.

Campaigns which alienate the organisation's supporters, antagonise policy-makers or involve high expenditure with little result are unlikely to be justifiable.

STRATEGIC PLANNING

Trustees have a responsibility to identify and communicate the overall mission of the organisation. This mission has to be consistent with but is not the same as the charitable objects. It provides a focus for the original vision of the founder or founders as interpreted by the present trustees.

On this basis, trustees can take an active part in collaboration with staff, trustees and other stakeholders in clarifying aims and objects and leading to the preparation of a development or business plan for the organisation.

Statement of the RNID's vision

The RNID's vision is to enable deaf people to exercise their rights to full citizenship.

Our understanding of citizenship is guided by the RNID's four principles:

- Deaf people are full members of society. They have equal rights, should be afforded equal respect and must be able to exercise equal opportunities.
- Deaf people have a right to the language and mode of communication of their choice.
- Deaf people have a right to equality of access to information and full participation in society.
- In providing services, full account must be taken of deaf people and other consumers, their experiences, their value, their rights and their opinions.

The RNID operates primarily in the UK but will draw upon international perspectives to guide its work and will use its influence to achieve its vision in international forums.

The RNID will achieve its goals by engaging in the following actions:

- Providing direct services to deaf people;
- Raising awareness;
- Campaigning to secure the rights of deaf people;
- Providing advice and information;
- Undertaking research and development;
- Providing skills based on training;
- Developing models of good practice; and
- Raising money to assist its work.

The RNID prides itself on providing these services to the highest quality. This quality is sustained by:

- Ensuring a partnership between staff and members in setting and pursuing corporate objectives;

- Helping staff to have pride in their work and the work of the Institute as a whole;
- Motivating and involving staff and members;
- Using and generating resources wisely;
- Ensuring that staff have exemplary communication skills; and
- Making sure quality is monitored and evaluated.

The RNID will provide a working environment within which this can happen.

Resources to help the strategic planning of organisations – for example the charities group of the Strategic Planning Society, and those offering workshops and consultancy on strategic planning – should be directed as much at trustees as at the paid staff of voluntary organisations.

SUMMARY

This chapter has outlined the management responsibilities of trustees including discussion of:

- employment of staff;
- accountability;
- representation; and
- strategic planning.

Future chapters will consider how trustees can best be helped to perform these roles and responsibilities as effectively as possible.

9 Roles of honorary officers

INTRODUCTION

As an agency develops, an inner group of trustees becomes helpful, often necessary. This may consist of the chair, vice-chairs if any, treasurer, one or more professionals in relevant skills (for example property, medicine, education, equal opportunities) or sub-committee chairs. These may form a general purposes committee, an executive committee or simply be known as honorary officers. They are expected to be closer to day-to-day management, between full meetings of the board of trustees, to assist in preparing and sorting out issues in readiness for full Committee meetings.

For this 'two-tier' system to work constructively, without causing tension because other trustees feel 'left out', it is important that all concerned take care that communication is free and full. The inner group is advisory, without power of decision unless this power has been explicitly delegated.

THE CHAIR

The role of chair is time-consuming, with much work between meetings, representation of the organisation, and work with staff, in particular the chief executive. We estimate that for large charities this may involve as much as two or three days a week or even longer.

Chairing a large charity requires diplomatic and leadership skills of a high level. The central responsibilities of the chair are firstly 'ministerial responsibility', with a duty to defend the staff if something goes wrong, and, secondly, continuing responsibility to ensure that the Committee of trustees is properly consulted and works well.

THE HONORARY TREASURER

The role of treasurer is also demanding and time-consuming, with critical involvement in major financial decisions, and involves chairing a finance committee or, in smaller organisations, doing the financial work, including the book-keeping.

Treasurers may also find themselves held responsible for unpopular decisions which go against the perceived values of the organisation, preventing the adoption of policies which the organisation cannot afford.

The treasurer has therefore to have technical expertise appropriate to the scope and size of the organisation and sufficient authority with fellow trustees and other stakeholders in the organisation. S/he also needs skills in the assessment of risk (a skill acquired not only by training but also through experience).

OTHER HONORARY OFFICERS

Other individual honorary officers can be expected to lead on their own specialism, carrying their colleagues with them. The same may apply to other trustees with special skills, who are called in 'ad hoc' without being members of the inner group.

The exercise of leadership is of particular importance in the management of change. It is for consideration within organisations whether this should be seen as a particular responsibility of the honorary officers.

SUMMARY

In this chapter we have discussed the role of the honorary officers, including the chair and the honorary treasurer.

Particular attention should be paid to the advice, support and training needs of the honorary officers.

PART THREE
Learning from others

10 Relevant experience from other sectors in the UK

INTRODUCTION

There is much to learn from the efforts of other authorities to provide for volunteers or non-executive professionals in other sectors. In this chapter we examine the experience of training school governors, local authority councillors and non-executive directors.

SCHOOL GOVERNORS

The responsibilities of school governors were transformed by two Education Acts of 1986 and 1988. For the first time, governors were given statutory duties to help the head teacher in a number of ways, including deciding school policy, selecting staff and allocating school finances, as well as in matters of the curriculum, discipline, looking after the buildings and preparing an annual report for parents.

Perhaps the most radical change was the allocation of budgets to individual schools, known as the local management of schools initiative (LMS).

The LMS structure makes governors responsible for ensuring that their school's spending is kept within the budget and also for planning.

The most forward looking local education authorities (LEAs) have set up resource centres for schools. These provide materials for use by a pool of experienced trainers drawn from local colleges of further education or semi-retired professionals. Training covers equal opportunities, selection and recruitment techniques, aspects of curriculum development and school development planning. Ideally, these training programmes, delivered either on school premises or community training centres, are provided in a variety of formats, including evening, half-day and one-day sessions, but there is seldom such choice.

Contact and liaison with new governors is often channelled through a 'link' governor chosen by the LEA from the existing board. These people are responsible for ensuring that new members' learning needs are met, although in practice, the role of link governors is often ill-defined. Most LEAs also provide a written guide for new members and a regular newsletter.

While the needs of parent governors is provided directly by the schools, with support from the LEA, co-opted governors from the private sector have a further source of support in the Industrial Society.

Many LEAs are worried that the increased responsibility and time needed for the posts may mean many of the present governors declining re-election. The Department of Education and Science is currently engaged in a major campaign to encourage more parents and business people to volunteer.

A major plank of the campaign is being aimed at companies. The Industrial Society suggests a number of ways in which companies can encourage and support employees who already are or who wish to be governors. These include:

- publicising the idea and encouraging school governors through company newsletters etc;
- allowing employees paid time off to undertake governor duties;
- sponsoring employees on Industrial Society training programmes;
- encouraging reasonable use of the company's facilities (for example postage or photocopying); and
- positively encouraging employees who might not consider themselves senior enough to undertake governor duties.

Many companies are now taking up the challenge. British Gas, IBM (UK) Ltd and Esso, for example, allow up to five days per year to be taken as paid time as governors – for directors and shopfloor workers alike. Some companies have, by contrast, allowed time off in lieu for such public duties.

LOCAL AUTHORITY COUNCILLORS

The role of local authority councillor is, like those of school governors, under review.

Most training of councillors takes place within the authority. Many councils hold open days for newly elected councillors, which allow the various departments to explain their responsibilities.

Formal training is often provided in the form of evening or half-days sessions covering new developments in professional services and teaching skills such as rapid reading, chairing meetings, selection, interviewing and equal opportunities awareness. Wherever possible, meetings are held outside formal working hours, which has been found to attract better attendance.

Training is generally co-ordinated by the personnel department of the authority, sometimes by an official called a members services officer. Guidance on training is provided by the Local Government Management Board (LGMB), which publishes an action planning booklet for training officers and a guide, *On Their Terms* (1988).

Formal training is also available from a variety of external agencies. These include:

- Representative bodies – such as the Association of Councillors (which provides study weekends for elected members) and the Local Government Information Unit;
- Institutions of higher education – such as the Institute of Local Government Studies at the Birmingham University and the School for Advanced Urban Studies at Bristol; and
- Professional institutions – such as the Chartered Institute for Public Finance.

Cost is a factor. Many councillors are reluctant to spend public money on their own development at a time when public spending is so restricted.

NON-EXECUTIVE DIRECTORS

The role of non-executive directors (NEDs) of private companies is the subject of much current discussion in industry and commerce. Many institutional investors are calling for the role for the board to be strengthened, with the role of the chief executive and chairman separated and a majority of NEDs exercising greater influence on corporate policy-making.

The representative body for NEDs, ProNed, estimates that the number of board seats occupied by non-executive directors has increased from around a third to just under a half since 1985. Of Britain's largest 200 companies, ProNed claims, 99 per cent have 'a sound representation of non-executive board members'.

Some companies are now providing NEDs with opportunities to play a greater role in policy-making. The pharmaceutical company SmithKline Beecham, for example, has gone to considerable lengths to ensure that its NEDs acquire in-depth knowledge of its business. Two NEDs are assigned to each of the company's four core commercial activities – pharmaceutical, animal health, consumer brands and clinical laboratories – so that they come to understand enough of the business to conduct what the chairman describes as 'penetrating interrogation of management'.

However, the main source of formal development for NEDs in the UK is provided by the Institute of Directors. The IOD has argued for some time that directors, whether non-executive or executive, do not receive sufficient education. To remedy this problem, the Institute has set up the Centre for Director Development. Most of the courses are one or two days' long. Particularly relevant to NEDs is a course which covers company strategy, boardroom team-working, and the legal liabilities and fiduciary responsibilities of company directors.

RELEVANT LEARNING POINTS

Flexible delivery

All learning providers, including the Industrial Society, the LGMB and the Institute of Directors, stress the need for formal training or induction to be available in a variety of formats.

Training is best undertaken by local centres. But many local officials lack the experience and the resources to deliver courses or programmes unless they have the support of an expert body. The role of LEAs (in the case of school governors) and the LGMB (in the case of local councillors) is critical in providing:

- a framework of learning which can be easily adapted by local centres;
- education materials, for use on their own or as part of a course, including guidebooks, information packs, slides and action plans; and
- a pool of expert trainers which can act as a resource to be brought in when required.

Most potential or existing trustees, like school governors, local councillors and NEDs, are busy professionals and/or parents with child-care responsibilities. Evening or one-day courses at weekends are likely to be preferred options. In regions where volunteers have to travel a long way to attend meetings, the experience of the LGMB shows that residential weekends are also popular.

Action learning

All learning providers stress that programmes, courses or guided learning should be participative, involving group discussion, role playing and imaginative forms of action learning.

Closer co-operation with staff

In the case of both school governors and local councillors, the need to establish a close working relationship with paid staff is essential if volunteers are to carry out their responsibilities effectively.

The role of private sector sponsorship

The role of industry in encouraging more employees to become school governors, and to subsidise and support their development, provides a valuable precedent in any campaign to recruit trustees. Companies could be encouraged to promote trusteeship among their staff; allow employees paid time off to undertake their duties (IBM allow their staff to spend half a day a week on voluntary sector or community activities); sponsor them on courses; and provide subsidised facilities. A key role could be played by bodies such as the Industrial Society or the CBI or the Institute of Directors, in promoting a campaign to attract more trustees from industry and in providing workshops and programmes to help trustees understand their role.

SUMMARY

This chapter has examined the experience of volunteer or non-executive managers in three related fields:

- school governors;
- local authority councillors; and
- non-executive directors.

In each case there are many valuable lessons to be learned and applied in the context of charity trustees and committee members – not only in terms of the content and delivery of training, but also in terms of the investment and commitment required.

11 Non-profit Boards in the US

INTRODUCTION

The role of trustees on what are referred to as 'non-profits' in the United States has been given much more explicit recognition in the US than in England. Evidence for this can be seen in the range of publications produced specifically for Board members; in the increase in research on non-profit Boards over the last 10 years; and in the creation of the National Center for Non-profit Boards (NCNB) in 1988, which aims to improve the effectiveness of non-profit organisations by strengthening their governing Boards.

DEFINITION OF A GOOD BOARD

One piece of US research asked executive directors to define what they felt were the characteristics of a 'good Board'. The 12 characteristics with the highest scores were as follows:

1 The Board understands its legal responsibilities as the governing body of the organisation.
2 The Board president runs meetings in an effective and efficient manner.
3 The Board actively promotes the organisation to the community.
4 The Board takes an active part in long-range strategic planning for the organisation and is willing to embrace changes suggested by the planning process.
5 The Board chooses new members with regard to the specific skills and/or connections they can offer.
6 Board members prepare for meetings by reading material sent to them before the meeting.
7 Board members are willing to accept positions of leadership on the Board (officer, committee chairs).
8 Board members review financial statements carefully and ask for explanations of anything they do not understand.
9 The Board opens doors to possible funding sources for staff to pursue.
10 The Board stays out of administration, which is the executive's job.

11 Each Board member actively participates on at least one Board committee.
12 Board members are available between meetings when the executive needs to confer with them.

The research found a high correlation between those executives with 'good Boards' and those who invested time and effort in the recruitment and orientation of their Board members. (Research by Kathleen Brown Fletcher, University of San Francisco, presented to the Independent Sector's Spring Research Forum on 'Leadership and Management', March 1991).

CHANGING ROLES OF BOARDS

Traditionally US Boards have played a key role in fundraising for the organisation. The maxim 'give, get or get off' exemplifies this approach. Board members are not only expected to raise money, but also to give donations themselves.

However, with non-profit organisations increasingly providing services on a contract basis, there is some evidence that Board members have begun to play a bigger role in helping establish links with government agencies, developing partnerships and securing contracts.

US Standards

The National Charities Information Bureau (NCIB) assesses national not-for-profit organisations according to nine basic standards and informs potential funders through its reports about individual agencies. Each report includes a statement on the agency's aims, its activities, the name of the chair and chief executive, an analysis of its financial statements, salary ranges and current budgets. In addition, the NCIB comments on the performance of the organisation and its adherence or otherwise to its standards.

Board governance is listed as the first and most important indicator of an agency's health and effectiveness. It states, 'The Board is responsible for policy setting, fiscal guidance and ongoing governance and should regularly review the organisation's policies, programs and operations.' According to the NCIB, a Board should have

1 an independent volunteer membership;
2 a minimum of five voting members;
3 an individual attendance policy;
4 specific terms of office for its officers and members;
5 in-person, face-to-face meetings at least twice a year, evenly spaced with a majority of voting members in attendance at each meeting;
6 no fees to members for Board service, but payments may be made for expenses;
7 no more than one paid staff person member, usually the chief staff officer, who shall not chair the Board or serve as treasurer;
8 policy guidelines to avoid material conflicts of interest involving Board or staff; and
9 no material conflicts of interest involving Board or staff.

The NCIB now insists that these practices are written down and become official Board policy, not just 'how things are done'. Many agencies have responded to these conditions by taking the opportunity to review all their other Board policies and terms of reference.

The president of the NCIB said, 'Not only the health of each individual charitable organisation but the health of philanthropy as a whole rests on public trust in the ethics and practices of governing Boards. From what we have seen recently, that trust continues to be well placed.'

Another insight into the changes taking place in non-profit Boards in the US was provided by Geneva Johnson in her address to NCVO's Annual Conference in November 1990. Faced with a reduction in government grants at the same time as federal policy requires higher levels of activity and expansion, non-profits are having to rely increasingly on earned income. These changes have resulted in what she calls a 'new wave' of Board members. 'Traditional' Board members tend to be programme-orientated, co-operative with other organisations, broadly knowledgeable, generous with their time, mission-orientated, interested in quality and focused on the organisation. 'New-wave' Board members, on the other hand, tend to be data-orientated, entrepreneurial, specialised, limited with their time, results-orientated, interested in efficiency and focused on the organisation's operating environment.

Geneva Johnson notes that these shifts in Board members' perspectives have spawned problems for executives in, for example, maintaining cohesion, satisfying motivations of Board members and determining 'what is of value'. It is also interesting to see that there appears to be no place for the user on the new-wave boards. User involvement is viewed in terms of consumer research and citizens' rights rather than direct participation in governance. This is an interesting difference between the philosophy, if not always the practice, of the voluntary sector in the two countries.

ISSUES BEING RAISED IN THE US

At the Independent Sector's 1991 Spring Research Conference, the Executive Director of the National Center for Non-profit Boards identified seven key issues which she thought required further investigation.

1 To what extent are minorities represented?
2 Is there any evidence to confirm reports that younger people are showing less interest in contributing to non-profit organisations, whether as volunteers, donors or Board members?
3 Research is needed to demonstrate the wide spectrum of non-profit organisations which can be effective and to pick out the factors which seem to account for their success.
4 Who sits on non-profit Boards (age, sex, race, class)?
5 What can be learned from unconventional models of non-profit organisations, such as those where board members are paid?
6 What prompts Board members to scrutinise their performance as a Board and why do some never do this?
7 What is the relationship between the 'effectiveness' of the Board and the 'effectiveness' of the organisation it governs?

MANAGEMENT IMPLICATIONS OF CONTRACTS

Managing contracts presents as many challenges to voluntary organisations as it does to government agencies. One result of these management challenges in the US appears to have been a significant shift of responsibility away from the voluntary Committees towards professional staff.

Some US commentators argue that users and local people have no place on Committees but are better involved in advisory groups or as service providers. Others argue that a balance needs to be maintained on Committees between professionals and users and that the position of a voluntary organisation in negotiation with government is greatly strengthened if users are seen to be actively involved. This is certainly likely to be the case in England and therefore one of the conclusions to draw from US experience is the importance of finding appropriate ways of involving users – given the danger that the contract culture could result in their exclusion from playing any role at all in the contract process, other than being the passive recipient of services.

Some of the main conclusions from experience of

contracting in the US are therefore as follows:

- Committees of voluntary organisations should ensure they retain control of the strategic decision as to whether or not to enter into a contract, basing their assessment on its relationship to the organisation's mission.
- Committees should encourage voluntary organisations to become more businesslike in their contract negotiations and costing.
- The composition of Committees should maintain a balance between users and local people on the one hand and business and professional people on the other.
- Voluntary organisations should give priority to ensuring appropriate ways of involving users in planning, managing and monitoring service provision.

THE NATIONAL CENTER FOR NON-PROFIT BOARDS

One of the most significant developments in trustee training in the US was the establishment of the NCNB in 1988.

NCBN offers three programmes and services to meet the governance needs of the non-profits:

1 The Board Development Consultation Service helps non-profits design and conduct board development workshops and retreats, tailored to their board members and chief executives, and provides speakers for conferences and meetings.
2 The Board Information Center is a nationwide service that responds to written and telephone enquiries on a broad range of topics affecting non-profit boards.
3 The Publication Programme offers booklets, papers, books, audio tapes and other material on governing non-profits.

Now in its fourth year of operation NCNB has organised and conducted Board development programmes for over 60 non-profits. In addition thousands of non-profits have purchased over 50,000 Center publications. The Board Information Center has provided advice and referrals to thousands of non-profit professionals and volunteers seeking information on governance-related issues.

Examples of different kinds of support available

Examples of some of the publications produced by the Independent Sector include its nine-part Non-profit

Management Series covering:

1 The role of the Board and Board members;
2 Finding, developing and rewarding good Board members;
3 Operating effective committees;
4 Conducting good meetings;
5 The roles and relationships of the chief volunteer and the chief staff officers, Board and staff: Who does what?
6 Recruiting, encouraging and evaluating the chief staff officer;
7 Fundraising;
8 Budgeting and financial accountability; and
9 Evaluating results.

Other Independent Sector publications include *The Board Member's Book: Making a difference in voluntary organisations* and *Governance is Governance*, which spells out in a question-and-answer format what governance means and how board members can and will measure up to their responsibilities.

Some of The National Center for Non-profit Boards' resource materials include a two-hour audio cassette 'Building an Effective Non-profit Board', which highlights the vital role that Board members play in the success of non-profit organisations, and an eight-part series of booklets covering:

1 Ten basic responsibilities of non-profit Boards;
2 The chief executive's role in developing the non-profit Board;
3 Fundraising and the non-profit Board member;
4 Board assessment of the chief executive; a responsibility essential to good governance;
5 The non-profit Board's role in risk management; more than buying insurance;
6 Strategic planning and the non-profit Board;
7 Board passages; three key stages in a non-profit Board's life cycle; and
8 Understanding non-profit financial statements; a primer for Board members.

The Center currently has eight staff and was started with a launching grant from the WK Kellogg Foundation. It is now supported by a further 10 trusts and foundations, as well as generating income through its own services.

SUMMARY

In this chapter we have:

- stressed the higher priority given to training in the US and the wide range of resource material developed for trustees;
- discussed a US definition of 'a good Board';
- examined the way in which the role of Boards is

changing, particularly as a result of the 'contract culture';

- considered some of the main issues currently being raised concerning Boards in the US;
- noted the establishment of the NCNB in 1988.

There are two main implications for England arising from this review. The first is that we have a long way to go in this country in terms of developing resource materials and appropriate forms of support for trustees. There is much that we can learn from US experience in this respect.

The second important implication is that there are a number of factors in the current and future policy environment which are likely to diminish the role of the voluntary Committee in relation to paid staff and other professionals. These considerations are particularly relevant to the larger voluntary organisations in our society. All those involved in the voluntary sector in this country have to decide whether we want to follow this path.

PART FOUR
Content and approach

12 What trustees need to know

INTRODUCTION

It should be emphasised that trustees do *not* have to be experts in all the different subjects outlined in Part Two of our report. They can employ staff with this expertise or they can consult external advisers. What *is* important is that they are aware of their responsibilities and understand what questions they should be asking and the advice they should be seeking. In order to be able to do this there are certain basic areas with which trustees need to be familiar.

Our summary of what trustees need to know is drawn from a wide range of evidence. In particular, we have drawn on evidence submitted by the Association of Chief Executives of National Voluntary Organisations (ACENVO) and by consultants to the Inner Cities Unit, the Department of Trade and Industry, by three providers of training – the Directory of Social Change, the Charities Network and Action Resource Centre, Bristol. Specialist legal and financial advisers – the Industrial and Common Ownership Movement (ICOM), Bates, Wells & Braithwaite, the Legal Team at NCVO, BDO Binder Hamlyn, and Buzzacott & Co have also provided us with very helpful suggestions about what trustees need to know.

The chair, treasurer and other honorary officers of voluntary organisations have a particular duty to familiarise themselves with these subject areas and encourage other trustees to do likewise. The subject areas outlined are equally relevant to the members of management committees of voluntary organisations that are not charities.

It also should be stressed that trustees have also to look beyond their legal responsibilities, important as these are, to consider their broader responsibility for the 'governance' or overall guidance of the organisation.

ORGANISATIONAL CONTEXT

Trustees with a business or public sector background need an introduction to where their organisation fits into the voluntary sector. This overview should include information about relevant networks, for example in mental health, the environment, arts and museums, which may be particularly relevant to the organisation, as well as information about current funders and potential funding sources.

This will help to give the necessary perspective in thinking strategically on policy issues. Relationships with other voluntary organisations, statutory agencies and the business sector are open to misunderstanding. It is also important that trustees are in a position to be able to respond to changes both in and outside their organisations – and to be able to manage change rather than being managed by it.

LEGAL RESPONSIBILITIES

The legal responsibilities, duties and liabilities of trustees, including the implications of being a charity and of being a corporation, and an awareness of governing instruments, are essential knowledge.

Authoritative advice is often needed on the legal basis for trustee actions, especially where their governing instruments say nothing or are unclear. For example many trustees feel worried about the extent of their personal liability in a wide range of circumstances and liability under the Insolvency Act 1986. This needs to be clearly explained.

FINANCIAL RESPONSIBILITIES

Trustees have to understand the finances of their organisation, whatever its size and complexity.

- They need to be able to read budgets and accounts, and have some understanding of accounting practices (for example SORP 2).
- They need to know how to draw up or assess a development (or business) plan for their organisation, and to ensure that the organisation has the management capacity to carry through a business plan.
- Where the organisation has assets, financial reserves or property, the trustees need to know enough to use

professional advisers efficiently. The same applies to questions of tax and VAT liability.

Training trustees in their investment role

Overseeing investments is an important duty of trustees, and they need training if they want to operate in confidence in this highly specialised area. A firm of brokers, Bacon & Woodrow, have devised a training programme as a first step. Their specimen training agenda includes the following:

Topic	Subjects covered
Course introduction	Objectives, structure, assessment
The investment role of charity trustees	1 The overall role of a board 2 The investment decision-making process ('investment role') 3 Constraints: legal requirements: TIA, Trust Deed
Setting investment objectives	1 The role of budgeting 2 Setting current and planning future expenditure (recognising effect of inflation) 3 Setting benchmarks
Investment securities and markets	1 Shares, property, fixed interest –what are they? –income, risk and return characteristics 2 Investment portfolios –need for diversification –need for exposure to 'real assets'
Investment structures	1 Pooled funds a Common investment funds and b Authorised exempt unit trusts –what they can invest in –TIA status –fees –availability
Selecting fund managers	1 Fund management companies –role in finance industry –types by industry –services offered –institutional v private client 2 Selection criteria – what to look for 3 The selection process –shortlist –preparatory information –'beauty parade' 4 Administration –setting objectives and powers of –investment –form filling
Performance measurement	1 Meaningful comparisons 2 Using an accepted performance methodology and measurer
Monitoring fund managers	1 The need for monitoring –changes in client base, personnel, structure or style of the manager –impact on the manager's ability to provide a good service 2 How to monitor –assess the portfolio –regular contact with the manager –interpreting performance.

Trustees also need to be able to monitor actual spending and income against budget estimates and to identify, or ask their staff to identify, corrective action when required.

As well as knowing how to manage finances, trustees must be able to help raise money and to be confident that the organisation is approaching fundraising in a legal, efficient and effective manner.

Training trustees in fundraising

Some fundraising training opportunities do currently exist for trustees but where they do, they tend to exist as an adjunct to training courses provided for all members of staff. The Directory of Social Change, Institute of Charity Fundraising Managers, NCVO, Industrial Society and other independent training bodies all provide both general and specialist courses covering different aspects of fundraising. However there is a further need for training designed to give trustees a general background to the role of fundraising and more specific information on the interaction of different fundraising techniques and their effect on the management process of the whole organisation.

The trustee training on fundraising that currently does take place is often dependent on the initiative of the staff of the organisation rather than on directly approaching trustees themselves.

A number of national voluntary organisations now run in-house training schemes on fundraising both for staff and trustees. However, training in smaller organisations would necessarily require the use of outside training agencies.

Such a training programme would concentrate on a general overview of the place and purpose of fundraising and of the effect of differing types of fundraising upon budgets, cost:income ratios and likely results. It would also explain those aspects of fundraising activity that are strictly regulated by law.

Within an overall induction programme for trustees sufficient time must be given clearly explaining how fundraising fits into the organisation as a whole and the specific legal requirements of trustees to ensure that it is undertaken in a legal, ethical, efficient and effective manner.

There is anxiety in voluntary organisations of all shapes and sizes, where specific fundraising committees are established, if staff and trustees do not have a clear notion of their specific roles and obligations.

RESPONSIBILITIES FOR STAFF

Trustees are employers and so need to know about recruitment procedures, supervision and discipline. They are also responsible for the implementation of equal opportunities policies.

They may be involved in staff selection and interviewing, support and motivation of staff, and may have to develop and approve written conditions of service, disciplinary procedures and redundancy arrangements. Decision-making and conflict resolution in voluntary organisations often require considerable skills in the management of people, both staff and volunteers.

RESPONSIBILITIES FOR PROPERTY

Trustees are often responsible for properties and must therefore either employ staff with the expertise to manage properties or must develop that expertise themselves. Therefore, they need to be familiar with relevant legislation including licensing laws, insurance and planning and building regulations as well as being aware of their management responsibilities, for example in relation to security, maintenance and access.

STRATEGIC PLANNING AND EVALUATION

Trustees need to identify the organisation's values and how these influence its practice. They have to be able to explain the organisation's mission and strategic objectives. They need skills in forward planning, target setting and performance review. These skills are needed for all trustees and committees, so that they can have a commitment to a strategy, which they have developed, separate from day-to-day administration.

Evaluation of the organisation's performance is a particularly important task for trustees, which involves expertise in being able to monitor work programmes and progress in relation to targets, objectives and outcomes.

STRATEGIC MANAGEMENT AND ACCOUNTABILITY

Strategic planning and evaluation are essentially internal management processes, with leadership from trustees. At the same time trustees may need to steer the organisation's relationships with others, including policy-makers, funders, members, users and other voluntary organisations. Trustees, therefore, need to be aware of what is involved in effective representation and campaigning, as well as being aware of the processes for ensuring accountability to key stakeholders.

WORKING STRUCTURES AND RELATIONSHIPS

Trustees need to know the structure of their own organisation and its resources, mechanisms for trustee involvement, staff involvement, and reporting methods.

Another area of competence is less to do with the need for knowledge and more about the need to be able to develop effective relationships – for example within a committee or between the Committees and staff of the organisation.

Trustees have to understand what is involved in forming and running a Committee, and what a Committee is supposed to do. They also need to be able to work as a team, to move the organisation forward and to manage a staff team, setting a clear division of responsibilities between trustees and staff.

Clarification of the 'contract' and 'job description' of trustees with the organisation is also required. Trustees also need to be able to evaluate their own contribution to the effectiveness of the organisation, both as individuals and as a group.

SUMMARY

We recognise that what trustees need to know depends in part on the type of organisation in which they are involved. Nevertheless, there are certainly common areas of competence which all trustees need to have.

In this chapter we have outlined eight different subject areas with which trustees need to be familiar. Training courses and resource materials need to ensure that they cover these important topics.

RECOMMENDATIONS

1 Resource material and training provision for trustees should clearly state the main roles and responsibilities of charity trustees, highlighting the particular roles and responsibilities of the chair, treasurer and other honorary officers.
2 Advice, support and training for trustees should cover the following eight subject areas:

  – organisational context;
  – legal responsibilities;
  – financial responsibilities;
  – responsibilities for staff, where relevant;
  – responsibilities for property, where relevant;
  – strategic planning and evaluation;
  – strategic management and accountability; and
  – working structures and relationships.

These should cover the full range of their roles and responsibilities and not be limited to their legal responsibilities.

13 How trustees need to learn

INTRODUCTION

Throughout our work we have been struck by the resistance of trustees to the concept of training. Just under half the trustees in our survey felt that, while training was 'a good thing' there were no obvious or immediate needs relating to their own organisations. A substantial number felt that training was probably appropriate for some of the other trustees, but, by implication, not for themselves. Only one trustee in eight had experienced training directly related to his/her work as a trustee.

We believe this is very largely a problem of terminology and approach. Although a trustee might be reluctant to attend a training course for trustees, s/he might happily take part in a strategic planning meeting, attend a briefing on charity law or participate in the organisation's internal review. Yet, in each case, the result might be an increase in the person's effectiveness as a trustee.

We therefore think it is important to adopt a broad approach to the training of trustees both in terms of content and delivery. It is also important to recognise that paid staff need training in how to work effectively with trustees.

TAKING A BROAD VIEW OF TRAINING

While training courses are useful for the development of specific skills, trustees have to demonstrate qualities of leadership, judgement, and a strategic approach to the management of their organisations.

Taking a narrow view of training needs will not address the real issues that trustees and committees face. As we heard in evidence from 'Common Knowledge':

Increased proficiency, competence and technical know-how resulting from training in specific skills are distinct from the responsibilities accepted, understood and acted upon by trustees. These are not skills and cannot be developed by the 'instrumental' approach of training techniques. Trustees' responsibilities are in fact incompatible with being narrowly specialised because they depend on the formation of judgements, making decisions and thinking critically about new situations. Seeking the solution to a particular problem is different from being proficient in 'problem-solving'.

From this perspective, trustees cannot easily be trained to

- hold the ultimate power and authority in relation to all aspects of the work of a charity;
- act rationally, sensibly and carefully in financial matters;
- have a commitment to, and understanding of, the charity's work and its vision;
- be responsible for setting targets, standards and working methods of the organisation, and for being ready to adapt these as circumstances change; and
- have a continuing duty to what may be called the vitality of the organisation.

And yet these responsibilities are fundamental to a voluntary organisation. Therefore we have to find ways of enhancing the understanding as well as the knowledge of trustees.

Evidence from projects funded under the Advancing Good Management scheme stressed how important it is to involve the whole Committee. They acknowledged the difficulty of getting people to go on courses, and stressed the need to find a point of entry – for example through organisational reviews. They advocated a developmental approach which aimed to build on the strengths of a Committee and had a starting-point of identifying the vision of the organisation. Helping trustees to learn from each other, on the job, is an important part of this approach. Training can sometimes be fitted in to the regular cycle of Committee meetings.

A small organisation's approach to trustee training

Bransholme Women's Centre is a new project on an outlying estate in Hull. Established with Opportunities for Volunteering money, they have incorporated many aspects of good committee practice from the beginning. As they had funding for training earmarked in their grant, they began with the small group of women who made up the first management committee. Some women had no experience of acting as trustees and there were no governing instruments, policies or procedures already in place.

The Centre brought in an outside facilitator to help them develop committee skills such as chairing, minute-taking, and working together as a team and to boost their confidence. A worker described the process as being very flexible and starting from where the women were.

By the second session, though, it became quite a painful process with personality clashes needing to be sorted out. Once these had been resolved, we were able to set the basic groundrules, such as timekeeping, agendas and the work needed to be done between meetings. The facilitator built a strong foundation for the successful running of the group.

After the initial training sessions, the women felt more confident to attend outside courses on budgeting and financial planning. Later still, training sessions in the Centre were arranged to consider their financial and legal liabilities, their role as an employer, working with volunteers, and assertiveness training. According to the worker,

If training for the management committee is not in the budget, then it loses its priority. The centre is definitely reaping the rewards from induction and training and you can see the difference in the women.

Those giving evidence questioned whether many trustees would accept the idea of training for themselves. This was confirmed in our survey. It is important therefore to take a broad view of training, to include the opportunities for learning through induction processes, organisational reviews, information exchange, and other mechanisms for advice and support. It is also important to build training in as a routine activity, and not just as a response to a particular crisis or difficulty.

Some large charities' approaches to trustee training

A number of national charities have begun to tackle the issue of trustee training. At MIND, national council members are encouraged to attend one-day seminars on the principles of good committee management. The senior administrator shares the concerns of many of the charity's officers that new trustee members may need to know about their fiduciary duties, relating to the national organisation.

Increasingly we are getting user members on council as well as many representatives from the regions. All of them are keen to join because it brings them into the realm of national policy-making. But they often lack a clear understanding of their responsibilities and the extent of their personal liability should they fail to supervise and monitor the affairs of the charity effectively.

Additional training materials on the roles and responsibilities of trustees would be very welcome. These include distance learning materials that could be incorporated into the packs provided to new groups and could be used by the regional development officers on training days. Also, one-day seminars could be marketed to groups through MIND's newsletters or bought-in by the local associations.

Britain's largest children's charity, Barnardo's, has taken steps to ensure that Committee members understand their roles and responsibilities. Newly appointed members receive a two-page sheet outlining the legal requirements, but the chair feels that any trustee of a charity should be required to sign a statement stating that he or she understands the statutory obligations, which would, in turn, oblige charities to explain the personal liabilities involved.

The best way of explaining the importance of effective trusteeship would be by providing case-studies of crises which have occurred through poor stewardship. One-day seminars could be based around role-playing exercises in which participants would be placed in 'real-life scenarios' to explore the actions trustees would need to take in a crisis and to emphasise the importance of working closely with the charity's officers and paid employees.

The chair of Barnardos also feels that more focus should be provided to some of the ethical questions of charity management. 'How much should a charity spend on fundraising drives and on public relations? What aspects of a charity's work should be provided by volunteers and what by paid staff? How should the Committee judge whether a charity is effective in achieving its goals and what criteria should be used in drawing up measures of effectiveness?'

Save the Children Fund has devised guidelines on the qualities and competencies needed in its trustee body. All new trustees spend a half day with the chief executive to discuss the roles and responsibilities, the Fund's expectations, time requirements, aims and objectives. The intention is that all trustees should fully understand the mission and mandate of SCF and be able to stand up in public and express an understanding of the charity.

The chief executive feels that the trustee board must fully reflect all the interests and needs of the charity and that it should include a wide spectrum of all the experience and knowledge required by the charity. Where charities are unable to attract trustees with the right background and experience needed to balance the Committee in this way, then training should be provided.

The Fund offers training opportunities for its trustees which may not be specific to their role as trustee, but may be a useful addition to their knowledge. These may be on how to chair a meeting and public speaking skills.

THE TAKE-UP OF TRAINING COURSES

The constraints on busy people who are involved with organisations in a voluntary management capacity are well known. Low rates of attendance on courses can be discouraging. Lack of time was cited by almost everyone in our survey as a 'block' to training. It is therefore essential to assess when and where training courses can most appropriately be held to meet this problem. Often, a different kind of approach will be needed. However, someone becoming a trustee for the first time is more likely to be prepared to attend a course.

Trainers need a thorough understanding of voluntary sector issues, problems and styles of operation, a commitment to equal opportunities and a sensitivity to language and values appropriate to the organisation. Action Resource Centre's Management Training Project has run a small pilot scheme involving the free use of trainers from the private sector for courses in time management and presentation skills. These involved careful preparation with the trainers to minimise differences of perception and to modify any inappropriate elements within the course content. These pilot courses were successful and future plans include extending the scheme to involve further companies.

Free training provided by ARC's Management Training Project has not been without its problems. Drop-out rates on courses were fairly high, with cancellations at the last minute (due to a sudden crisis in the organisations, understaffing or too heavy a workload, but also where staff made all the arrangements and had ownership of the training). Their experience is that free facilities are not highly valued, even sometimes where individualised training for trustees is concerned.

People lacking in confidence or motivation often derive a feeling of worth from receiving training. For this reason training courses should provide at least a certificate of attendance: those that feel they are above such things usually have other ways of confirming their status.

Each person brings different expertise to an organisation. An agreed list of competences, defining precisely what it is necessary to be able to do in order to carry out a particular activity, gives a checklist against which to evaluate the relevance of a person's previous experience, skills and knowledge and to identify gaps, for example in finance, or strategic issues in the voluntary sector. Whatever methods or approaches to training are adopted, they will need to be consistent with mainstream education and training developments. This includes National Vocational Qualifications (NVQ), the Assessment of Prior Experience and Learning (APEL) and Credit Accumulation and Transfer (CATS). CATS enables individuals to acquire credits from training which can be subsequently added to, either because of geographical or career mobility or personal development.

We have given examples in Chapter 12 of the sort of competences a trustee might be expected to possess. Moves towards the accreditation of training, for example the Royal Society of Arts certificate, and in the longer term a system of accreditation linked to the system of National Vocational Qualifications will be of benefit to trustees looking for recognition of their competences.

Competency-based approach

The RSA's Advanced Diploma in the Organisation of Community Groups has the following units and elements of competence:

Unit 1   Review and develop the activities of an organisation within the community
1 Produce a community profile which develops a clear concept of the community within which the group is operating.
2 Review the aims of the organisation.
3 Promote equality of opportunity within a community group.
4 Review the activities of the group over a period of time in the light of community information.
5 Develop and maintain contacts with other voluntary and statutory bodies.
6 Identify potential developments for the organisation.

Unit 2   Organise an event or programme of events
1 Define the objective(s) to be achieved.
2 Establish a timetable for planning and delivery.
3 Publicise and promote the event/programme.
4 Co-ordinate the carrying out of a plan for an event programme.
5 Evaluate and report on the success of the event/programme in terms of the original objective.

Unit 3   Manage financial resources
1 Explain the role of the treasurer.
2 Carry out simple bookkeeping procedures.

3 Establish budget heads for the group/organisation.
4 Draw up a budget for a specific activity.
5 Present a budget to members of the organisation.
6 Control, over a period of time, the budget drawn up for a particular activity.
7 Prepare for annual audit.
8 Report to a General Meeting or a committee meeting on the finances of the organisation.
9 Prepare an application for funding.

Unit 4   Manage material resources
1 Assess and acquire material resources for a project or activity.
2 Prepare and maintain an inventory.
3 Identify and assess the insurance requirements of a project or activity.
4 Ensure that health and safety standards are fulfilled for a project or activity.
5 Assess whether the organisation's activities are accessible to people with special needs.
6 Assess and report on the running costs of a project or activity.

OTHER CONSIDERATIONS

It is important in an organisation that all trustees are involved in training. This ensures that the less confident and experienced are not made to feel uncomfortable and also that those who may think they have nothing to learn are also exposed to new ideas.

Many trustees with a commercial background – including some who submitted evidence to us – do not see themselves as needing 'training'. Instead they identify a need for training with trustees without business experience (though such people may know more about the work of the charity). However, it would be unwise to assume that business experience, though useful, will necessarily prepare trustees for the different world of charity administration.

There is a danger that more experienced or qualified trustees may lack patience with those who are less well informed. They should recognise that they have a responsibility to keep fellow trustees informed on all matters, where they have collective responsibility. This applies in particular to the role of the chair and treasurer. It is also the responsibility of the other members of the Committee to ensure they are well informed about their own responsibilities as trustees.

Committee meetings are an opportunity – and should be used as such – to bring together the competences of trustees derived from their external experience to respond effectively to the needs of the charitable organisation.

CRITERIA FOR ASSESSING THE PROVISION OF TRAINING

We are concerned that resources for support and training of trustees should be accessible.

• Committees are unlikely to be willing (or often able) to afford full-cost training for themselves, and it is necessary to look for subsidy from funders as sponsors.
• Members of Committees are unlikely to have any spare time, in addition to their existing commitment, and so training and other support should as far as possible be fitted in with their existing commitments or delivered in ways which are economical of time and attractive in format.
• Written material must make use of that which is familiar and accessible.

Training materials and resources will only be relevant if they are based on an understanding of the trustees' need for clear information, while acknowledging potentially confused interpretation and judgement, and

• an appreciation of what trustees are supposed to do with the information;
• an appreciation that training has a negative image for some people and a positive image for others; and
• an awareness that a need for training may encompass a further need for consultation and advice.

SUMMARY

In this chapter we have discussed *the way* in which trustees need to learn – as opposed to *what* they need to learn. We have stressed the importance of taking a broad view of training.

We have also drawn attention to the problem of low take-up of training courses and suggested that certificates of attendance or systems of accreditation could help increase the status of training.

We have emphasised that all trustees, whatever their background, have something to learn as well as having something to teach each other.

Finally, we have suggested ways of assessing provision, so that trustees can decide for themselves whether a particular type of provision is likely to be helpful.

RECOMMENDATIONS

3 Training courses should be particularly targeted at inexperienced trustees and lead at least to a certificate of attendance and, where possible, to some form of accreditation of courses.

4 Training provision should be

– assessed for its accessibility in terms of time, cost and familiarity of language and approach; and

– fully accessible, for example through the provision of interpreters at meetings, including sign language interpreters for deaf people, sub-titles on videos, and translation into other languages, as required.

5 Committee meetings should be seen as opportunities for learning, and training elements and review processes built into the annual cycle of meetings.

14 Range of mechanisms required

INTRODUCTION

Our survey suggests that at present a minority of trustees receive any form of advice, support or training. Less than one trustee in ten recalled seeing the Charity Commission's leaflets. Just over one in eight had experienced training directly related to his/her work as a trustee. Just over one in five had been through a recognisable induction process and only one-third of local trustees (and half of national trustees) had received information about their own and their organisation's role or about their responsibilities as trustees.

Much of the fault for this must lie with the organisations themselves, and it is important to find ways of ensuring that trustees get support from their organisations. Nevertheless, there are considerable barriers to the provision of effective support to trustees. Some of these relate to the voluntary nature of the role and the lack of time available to trustees. Others relate to trustees' own perceptions of 'training', and others relate to the nature of the provision which is often inaccessible, inappropriate or non-existent.

We have therefore looked carefully at the range of mechanisms needed. No single mechanism will be sufficient on its own, but taken together, over time, we believe that our proposals would significantly improve the effectiveness of trustees. Responsibilities for implementing these mechanisms are discussed in Part Five.

We are impressed by the widely different contexts in which trustees have to work. Therefore we propose some general resources that would be useful for all trustees but argue that these should be reinforced by materials developed for specific purposes. Also, as busy people, trustees do not want to be faced with a comprehensive approach, covering all eventualities. They are more likely to be receptive to information and advice which they can see are relevant to their current situation.

INDUCTION

Our survey suggests that thorough induction is the single most important mechanism for supporting trustees, and without such preparation, it is very difficult for a trustee to perform his/her role or identify what further training would be useful.

The majority of respondents to our survey identified induction as a vital need. The following suggestions were made:

- New trustees should have detailed information on role, duties, legal and financial responsibilities of trustees, in clear, plain English. This should be available *before* they agree to become trustees.
- Written materials do not work well unless combined with an opportunity to discuss issues and information, through seminars, meetings, one-to-one briefings, and so on.
- Each organisation should provide a clear account of its purpose and history, the role of the Committee and how trustees fit in, and trustees' role in the funding of the organisation. This could be included on the cover of a trustee folder, as a constant reminder.
- Induction should include 'team building' with all the trustees, to develop a Committee that works well.

Further details about recommended induction arrangements are given in Chapter 16.

TRAINING COURSES

We welcome the development of one-day seminars and short courses. They are useful both as a general introduction and to give up-to-date information on specific areas of knowledge and have proved popular with some trustees. However, many trustees have yet to be convinced of the usefulness of these events. We heard in evidence that having speakers from the Charity Commission improved attendance and we see potential for their increased involvement. Speakers from legal and accountancy firms are also a welcome development.

Some courses have been developed for trustees and paid staff to attend together, and we welcome this development as an acknowledgement of the shared interest of trustees and staff in the effective management of the organisation.

We are aware of the prohibitive cost of training courses for many small, local and rural organisations. We recommend that funders look sympathetically at applications for support, so that these courses may be subsidised (see Chapter 18).

Often the best training involves the whole Committee taking part together. We recommend that charities and voluntary organisations look at ways of setting up such training as a normal practice, budgeted for in the same way as their other regular activities.

VIDEOS, AUDIO-TAPES AND DISTANCE LEARNING

There is scope for videos, which may be used flexibly by Committees, or by individual trustees in their own time, and by those who are considering getting involved with a charity at this level. Videos can give a positive image to the management of charities and show what issues trustees have to handle. We therefore welcome initiatives to develop videos which will encourage trustees to recognise the importance of the issues with which they are working.

Examples of subjects which videos could usefully cover include:

- what managing a voluntary organisations means, an overview for new trustees;
- Committee-staff relationships – an introduction to the do's and don'ts; and
- effective Committees – along the lines of Video Arts' highly successful 'Meetings, Bloody Meetings'.

Audio-tapes have a use in specialist areas. Examples from the Center for Non-profit Organisations in the USA indicate the range of possible subjects.

We welcome the development of distance learning relating to voluntary Committees and see its advantages both in improving access to relevant information and expertise and also in accrediting learning. These mechanisms do, however, often require a substantial investment of time which not all trustees will be able to make.

LEAFLETS

The present leaflets produced by the Charity Commission are too lengthy to be relevant to all trustees. One respondent suggested that the Commission's leaflets were useful only after the organisation had grown: 'Early on they were irrelevant – too much! We wanted simple, practical help. Only later did they become useful.'

A simpler leaflet about the responsibilities of trustees is needed. It should include a clear and straightforward description of their legal powers and responsibilities. It needs to be written in a very accessible and user-friendly form, and very widely distributed.

HANDBOOKS

There is a need for general reference handbooks which are comprehensive and authoritative. These may be aimed at a particular sector, for example arts organisations, community trusts – and produced by, or in association with, their representative bodies – or aimed at trustees' work from a particular background, for example from the British Institute of Management. There is also a need for handbooks which are written with small organisations in mind, and for agencies with no staff.

Much of the content of such handbooks will be similar. It is important also that it is authoritative. We therefore recommend that a general handbook for trustees be produced in a form that can then be adapted and added to by particular networks or individual voluntary organisations.

The core content of the handbook should include sections on:

- recruitment of trustees;
- induction of trustees;
- information to be provided to trustees;
- the roles and responsibilities of trustees;
- the questions trustees should be asking;
- the critical issues trustees should be monitoring;
- the procedures trustees should be requiring (for example evaluation);
- relationships with paid staff;
- advice on growth and contraction of the organisation;
- criteria for assessing the provision of advice, support and training; and
- competencies for trustees.

The handbook should also contain a range of information about the individual network or organisation itself.

TRUSTEE SUPPORT SERVICES

Trustees need to be able to get advice and support in a variety of ways – from their own organisation, from the Charity Commission, from their network and from other agencies. However, there is a growing need for independent advice services particularly targeted at the needs of trustees.

These services would cover the full range of trustees' responsibilities and would provide independent advice and information. They could be delivered by a number of different national and local development agencies. At the same time there is a need for one agency to stimulate and help develop these services in a cost-effective manner.

SUMMARY

In this chapter we have discussed a range of mechanisms required for the effective support of trustees, including

- induction;
- training courses;
- videos, audio-tapes and distance learning;
- leaflets;
- handbooks; and
- trustee support services.

More detailed proposals for implementing these mechanisms are made in Part Five.

RECOMMENDATIONS

6 A range of different training courses should be developed to meet the needs of different kinds of organisation, for example community organisations with no staff, large national charities and organisations with significant capital assets. Joint training of trustees and staff should be included as part of any programme for organisations employing staff.

7 Distance learning initiatives, such as the Open University's new voluntary sector management course, need to be developed further and made accessible to the full range of trustees.

8 A general information pack for trustees and their organisations should be produced in a form that can then be adapted and added to by particular networks or individual voluntary organisations. The core content of the information pack should include sections on:

- recruitment of trustees;
- induction of trustees;
- information to be provided to trustees;
- the roles and responsibilities of trustees;
- the questions trustees should be asking;
- the critical issues trustees should be monitoring;

- relationships with staff, where relevant;
- advice on growth and contraction of the organisation;
- criteria for assessing the provision of advice, support and training; and
- competencies for trustees.

9 A development unit for trustee support services should be established to encourage and co-ordinate the development of a wide range of advice, support and training for trustees by other agencies (see Recommendation 24).

PART FIVE
Responsibilities for action

15 A framework for action

INTRODUCTION

The training and support of trustees must take account of their very different kinds of organisation. There is no one right approach; nor is any part of the voluntary sector to be excluded. The needs of Committee members of community organisations, of the trustees of small grant-giving trusts, and of chairs of large charities are different, but equally valid.

A framework for action has to be comprehensive, in recognition of the wide range of individuals and institutions who have a contribution to make in the support of trustees.

Training – or any other support – cannot be effective in isolation. In devising training opportunities it is necessary to examine assumptions about the recruitment and role of trustees.

Training and support have to take place within the context of the organisation. Standard packages of training have a limited use.

We have tried to learn as much as possible from the experience of other countries, such as the USA, and other related fields, such as school governors, local authority councillors and non-executive directors of companies.

RESPONSIBILITIES

Trustees themselves have the prime responsibility for ensuring high standards rather than having them imposed by external or statutory enforcement agencies. Nevertheless, a number of different agencies have important roles in helping trustees to discharge these responsibilities effectively.

Trustees' own organisations have the most important role, since they are in the best position to identify needs and take appropriate action. But where trustees are unaware of their position and responsibilities, or an organisation has no paid staff, they will need to be reminded of their responsibilities by the Charity Commission and other agencies. The Charity Commission, NCVO, central and local government, other funders and many other national and local agencies all

have a role to play in bringing this about.

We believe it is important that trustees know where they can go for help and advice; that they have a choice of avenues to pursue; and that provision is tailored to their needs. This is what our recommendations aim to achieve.

ACTION AT DIFFERENT LEVELS

Having made recommendations about the content and approach of training for trustees, it is important to identify 'who should do what'.

Our aim throughout has been to recommend action which will increase the effectiveness of trustees. In order to do this we have developed a framework for action comprising

- action by *organisations* to support their trustees;
- action by *agencies* providing advice and support;
- action by *government and other funders*; and
- action by *individual* trustees.

The remaining recommendations have been developed within this framework.

DEVELOPING AND ASSESSING PROVISION

Some of those giving evidence to the Working Party have suggested that a body, such as NCVO, should 'kitemark' the provision of advice, support and training for trustees to ensure it meets a specified standard. We do not think this is practicable or desirable, but we do see an important role for NCVO in issuing guidance on provision and in identifying criteria for assessing provision.

These criteria, which we recommend should be included in a trustees' handbook, would enable trustees and organisations themselves to judge whether a particular course, publication or other initiative was appropriate to their needs.

We also welcome the development of competence-based standards in certain kinds of committee work, as these will help in assessing the need for the development of support services and training resources.

RANGE OF INITIATIVES REQUIRED

An effective programme of support for trustees throughout the voluntary sector will require a number of separate initiatives to meet the particular needs of 'experts', those who are trustees because they are 'representatives', as well as taking full account of the demands of community organisations, specialist agencies providing professional services, campaigning organisations, and large charities with a high national profile and bureaucratic structures to support their diverse functions.

These separate initiatives will benefit from co-ordination and co-operation – for example in the development of information and advice services for trustees.

Some large charities have developed support services for their local branch Committees. Some local development agencies have also developed training for Committees. It is useful to build on this experience and to use the relevant networks to improve the quality of the support to be developed further within the voluntary sector, with the encouragement of outside agencies and funders.

This is seen as part of a process of self-regulation within the voluntary sector. In some instances we may see the emergence of objective measures of effectiveness – for example through accreditation and the application of competence-based standards to voluntary management.

SUMMARY

In this chapter we have outlined a framework for action at four different levels:

- the organisation itself;
- agencies providing advice and support;
- government and funders; and
- the individual trustee.

The rest of Part Five outlines the action we recommend at each level.

16 Action by organisations to support their trustees

INTRODUCTION

The organisation itself has a critical role to play in the provision of advice, support and training for trustees.

First, the organisation has a responsibility for ensuring the whole issue of trustee training gets on to the agenda. Then, its approach to recruitment of trustees, induction, the committee structures it develops, the support it provides, the status it accords its trustees (in practice rather than on paper), will all have a major impact on the effectiveness of trustees.

RESPONSIBILITIES

It is clear from those who have given evidence to the Working Party that one of the difficulties of trustee training is that no one sees it as their responsibility. We believe the prime responsibility for ensuring appropriate advice, support and training takes place rests with the organisation itself.

Where there are paid staff, the senior staff member should ensure that the issue is considered by the trustees. It is then the chair's responsibility to discuss with the other trustees what they want, having been advised by the senior staff member of the range of possible approaches and mechanisms available. The senior staff member is then responsible for implementing whatever they decide.

Where there are no paid staff, the chair has to be responsible at all stages of the process. In both cases adequate budget provision will have to be made for implementation.

RECRUITMENT

The recruitment of trustees is often carried out without clarifying what is expected of trustees. We heard evidence that telling people what is involved in being on a Committee has put them off, but this is preferable to finding out later that the responsibilities being asked for are beyond one's capacities of time, energy, or commitment.

The recruitment of trustees should be taken just as seriously as the recruitment of staff. There is a similar need to clarify the qualities being looked for (person specification) and the tasks that are required (job description).

Some charities with equal opportunities policies do not implement these policies effectively in relation to their own Committees. Committees should regularly review their practice – for example, time and venue for meetings – to see if they are discriminating against participation by actual or potential members.

In some instances there will be a need for attention to literacy needs, to language translation and interpretation, to hearing and sight disabilities, and so on. (Organisations such as the Royal National Institute for the Blind are aware of these issues and may be approached for help for specific advice and training.)

It is clear from our survey and other evidence that most of these procedures are not currently followed. This is part of the reason why trustees are so unrepresentative of the population as a whole in terms of age, class, gender, race, disability and other characteristics.

We heard evidence that recruitment is very often haphazard and ill thought out. We would recommend a more systematic approach, with a needs analysis in association with an audit of current strengths of the Committee.

Many of those giving evidence, including the Association of Chief Executives for National Voluntary Organisations (ACENVO), have emphasised the importance of job descriptions and a clear approach to what is needed:

> The development of job descriptions and person specifications for trustees would not only help actual or potential trustees to understand their role, but also serve as a tool to encourage potentially suitable individuals to come forward for election/selection. It would also highlight the (sometimes hidden) assumptions that influence this process at present and facilitate open debate about the skills and abilities that need to be represented.

The unclear way in which trustees are often recruited to the organisation may mean that they agree to serve as trustees because they want to be *involved* – to support its work – but they are not motivated to *manage* its affairs. This will change, if these expectations are made explicit at the time of recruitment.

A planned approach to recruitment will help the organisation to get the trustees it wants, but also it will help to explain to prospective trustees the responsibilities they are taking on and the expectations that others will have of them.

It will of course be much harder to apply these principles when trustees are elected by a particular constituency to serve on a Committee. Nevertheless, it is still important for the organisation to try and make clear, both to the constituency and to potential candidates for election, what kinds of tasks will be involved and what kinds of qualities are required.

INDUCTION

Induction was identified as a vital need by the majority of respondents to our survey. Yet only just over one trustee in five had been through a recognisable induction process. Roughly the same number again spoke of an informal induction system. The organisation has a good opportunity to influence a Committee member's approach to the work by giving emphasis to an induction programme.

We recommend that there be a systematic induction programme for new trustees. This should be linked to an annual cycle of planning review meetings, which will ensure that all trustees have the opportunity to be informed of current developments in the organisation. Some organisations have an induction meeting for newly elected trustees following the AGM. Such meetings should involve all trustees and relevant paid staff.

An induction programme should be linked to the production and updating of a trustee handbook. The handbook should include

- an up-to-date list of trustees of the charity (distinguishing, where necessary, between charity trustees and holding trustees and explaining the difference);
- an organisation chart and list of key staff, with job titles and a clear indication of their responsibilities;
- a statement of the responsibilities of trustees; this should include essential information from the Charity Commission;
- a statement of the constitution of the organisation, clearly describing the legal status, charitable objects,

and relevant information on the appointment or election of trustees; and
- the organisation's annual report and accounts.

The handbook should build on the core material of the trustee handbook referred to in Recommendation 8. All of this information should be in easy-to-read form, and state where the original documents are kept and may be examined. The handbook should also give a brief history of the organisation, and say if it is affiliated to any other organisation. The handbook may also include any other information on the organisation which is relevant to the work of trustees – for example on standards of service provision, and information systems. In any case, the trustees should consider the existing handbook on an annual basis and agree any up-dates required.

Induction procedures should include adequate time for discussion between new trustees, paid staff and experienced trustees. Discussion about current and forthcoming issues facing the organisation is just as important a part of induction as the provision of written material and briefings on the legal responsibilities of trustees.

The yearly cycle

A number of voluntary organisations have now adopted a yearly cycle of induction, training, planning and review involving all the Committee members. Shortly after the AGM and before the first formal Committee meeting, all members are brought together for a informal session in which they can get to know each other, the reasons for joining the Committee, to meet the staff, walk round the premises and to receive an induction pack.

At the induction gathering, the chair might express his or her hopes for the coming year, explain how the Committee works, when it meets, how to get items on to the agenda, and dates for the year.

A further, more formalised session is then arranged to offer the trustees training in their roles and responsibilities. This is done either by sending them on an outside short course or by arranging it within the organisation. Such a course would consider good meeting skills, effective decision-making processes and the basics of evaluation and monitoring.

At some point in the yearly cycle, the Committee then assesses the organisation's mission statement, its aims and objectives, the one-year plan, the budget, staff work targets and the composition and effectiveness of the Committee itself. In this organisational review, internal differences may well come to the fore, with conflicts resolved and decisions taken to move the charity on. Using straightforward evaluation techniques, the organisation can review its past performance and plan for the future.

This can be a painful, time-consuming and costly exercise, particularly the first time it is attempted. It may also require the help of an outside facilitator to assist the process. However, once the process is in place, organisations can quite comfortably conduct a planning and review day themselves.

Structures

Many organisations have structures and working methods that hinder the effectiveness of their trustees and Committees.

The size of the Committee can itself be a problem. This is not a matter for regulation, but Committees that are swollen for reasons of representation – for example with 30 members or more – may have difficulties in having a clear sense of purpose, focused debate and effective decision-making. In some cases organisations may find it useful to separate their consultative and management systems.

The effectiveness of trustees is intimately bound up in the relationship of the Committee with the organisation. The composition of the Committee will itself say something important about the nature of the organisation.

An equal opportunities policy

Equal opportunity policies of voluntary organisations mostly refer to the recruitment of staff and the users of the service. Great pains are often taken to ensure that individuals and groups are not discriminated against when applying for a staff post or in receiving the benefit of the organisation's activities.

One area which has been more consistently neglected is the application of the equal opportunities policy to the management committee itself. Ironically, it is the Committee who will approve the measures in the first place, but will often fail to apply it to the recruitment and makeup of its own members. Some organisations, such as Family Service Units, now make explicit reference to the Committee members in their Anti-Racist Policy Statement.

In its guidelines on equal opportunities, the Consortium on Opportunities for Volunteering suggest that in setting up a management committee groups should take the following into consideration:

- skills and experience relevant to the work of the project;
- fair representation of the local population in terms of gender, ethnic background, disability, age and class;
- appropriate statutory agency representation;
- other voluntary sector agency representation;
- the interests and views of volunteers working in the project; and

- the interests and views of service users.

In order to achieve a wide range of skills and experience a group may wish to have both co-opted and full members. The constitution or governing instrument should provide for this. Often the status of co-opted members differs from that of full members as they do not have full voting rights. To avoid tokenism, co-opted members from under-represented groups should be offered these rights.

The relationship of the chair and the senior staff member is often a key factor in integrating the Committee and staff contributions to the effectiveness of the organisation.

GOOD COMMITTEE PRACTICE

The procedures adopted by an organisation will have an impact on the contributions that individual trustees are able to make. It is helpful to discuss whether meetings are achieving the right balance of formality and decision-making with information-sharing and discussion of policy issues.

It is helpful to have specific terms of office, and a means of ensuring the succession to key roles, including that of chair.

The organisation may adopt a policy on attendance at meetings, so as to confront the issue of inactive members.

CONTINUING SUPPORT

Although good induction procedures are important for effective trusteeship, they should not be the sum total of the organisation's trustee training efforts. There is also a need for a rolling programme of advice, support and training based on an assessment of need.

The most effective training is often for the whole Committee. We recommend that charities and voluntary organisations look at ways of establishing such training as a normal practice, budgeted for in the same way as their other activities.

REINFORCEMENT AND REVIEW

We have already commented on our survey finding that only one trustee in three actually knew they were a charity trustee. Although this is partly a problem of terminology, we believe it reflects a wider problem, namely that the roles and responsibilities of trustees are not sufficiently central and explicit within the work of many charities. Trustees do not think of themselves as trustees, because their organisations often do not think of them as trustees either.

There are a number of ways this difficulty could be overcome – identifying trustees more clearly in annual reports and other publications, including a statement on the training provided to trustees and staff in annual reports, addressing them as trustees in correspondence and organising meetings, at least once a year, at which the trustees review and evaluate the organisation's overall work and set objectives both for themselves and for the organisation.

SUMMARY

In this chapter we have considered how charities can help their trustees to be effective through

- ensuring the senior staff member and/or chair take responsibility for ensuring the provision of appropriate advice, support and training for trustees;
- implementing recruitment and induction procedures;
- developing effective structures and good committee practice;
- providing ongoing support; and
- reinforcing and reviewing the role of trustees on a regular basis.

RECOMMENDATIONS

10 The senior staff member, or, where there are no paid staff, the chair, should:
   - ensure that the Committee considers the issue of training of trustees;
   - implement whatever is agreed; and
   - ensure that the organisation budgets for training of trustees in the same way as for other activities.
11 Charities should develop clear guidelines on what they expect of their trustees, both individually and collectively. These should include the expected time commitment, and 'job descriptions' for the chair, treasurer, other honorary officers, and ordinary members of the Committee (which should be complementary to those of the staff).
12 Charities should have a policy for the composition, recruitment and appointment of their Committee, and an equal opportunities policy covering both their services and the recruitment and appointment of their staff and committees.
13 All charities should give urgent attention to their induction arrangements for trustees, developing an induction policy and procedures including briefing meetings and the provision of an information pack, including:

- an up-to-date list of trustees of the charity (distinguishing, where necessary, between charity trustees and holding trustees –and with an explanation of the difference);
- an up-to-date list of any other committees or advisory groups, which might have an influence on the management or supervision of the workers of the organisation;
- an organisation chart and list of key staff, with job titles and a clear indication of their responsibilities;
- a statement of the responsibilities, where relevant, of non-executive directors of companies limited by guarantee;
- a statement of the responsibilities of trustees; this should include essential information from the Charity Commission;
- a statement of the constitution of the organisation, clearly describing the legal status, charitable objectives, and relevant information on the appointment or election of trustees; and
- the organisation's annual report and accounts.

The information pack should provide or be an opportunity to discuss a mission statement; include a statement of current objectives, and policies to achieve them; indicate any problems to be overcome; and describe external relations (including sources of funding and any conditions attached to funds).

This information pack should build on the core material referred to in Recommendation 8.

14 Charities should carry out regular assessments of the training needs of their trustees and ensure that there is a rolling programme of advice, support and training for them within the resources available.
15 Annual reports and other relevant publications should clearly identify trustees as trustees with a statement of the action that the charities have taken to provide training for both trustees and paid staff.
16 Charities should consider appropriate ways of reinforcing the status and responsibilities of their trustees, for example through addressing them as 'trustee' in correspondence.
17 Charities should hold at least one meeting annually, at which trustees review and evaluate the overall work overall of the organisation and set objectives for it and for themselves.

17 Action by agencies providing advice and support

INTRODUCTION

Although there are many things which charities can do to increase the effectiveness of their trustees, much of the responsibility for action lies with other agencies. There is no point in every individual organisation reinventing the wheel through developing its own resource materials and its own training programmes, when much of this can be done more efficiently by other agencies. Furthermore, many organisations simply do not have the resources or the capacity to develop such materials and programmes.

In this chapter, therefore, we look at what action is required by a range of different agencies to improve the provision of advice, support and training for trustees. In particular we consider the role of the Charity Commission, NCVO and other agencies in the voluntary, private and statutory sectors.

THE CHARITY COMMISSION

We believe that the Charity Commission has a key role to play in the provision of advice, support and training for trustees, in addition to its role in monitoring and enforcing the law. In particular, we have highlighted its role in providing information to trustees; its role in providing advice relating to charity regulation and the legality of charities' activities; in maintaining an overview of the provision of training, including giving support to the need to increase provision; and in participating in other agencies' training events..

We welcome the division of the work of the Commission into charity supervision and charity support. We feel that this should reassure charities and encourage them to seek advice from the Commission.

Our survey suggests that the Charity Commission's current range of explanatory leaflets is not reaching the vast majority of trustees. Some of those who had received them felt they were only useful after the organisation had grown. They wanted simple, practical help at the outset. There were also a number of issues where further guidance was needed.

One of the great potential benefits of computerising the Central Register is that the Charity Commission will be much better placed to communicate with individual charities and even with individual charity trustees, since charities will be obliged to inform the Commission of the names and addresses of their chairs when they make their annual returns.

We therefore recommend that the Charity Commission should produce a new basic leaflet aimed at potential and existing trustees, outlining the responsibilities and roles of trustees, in simple, accessible language. This should be sent to all charities, when they receive the new annual return, in sufficient quantity for each trustee to have one. Whenever the Commission is informed of new trustees, it should automatically send them a copy of the leaflet. It should also be sent to organisations which 'supply' large numbers of trustees such as local authorities and companies. Copies should also be available in local libraries, local development agencies, citizens advice bureaux and other outlets. The leaflet should also list other sources of advice available, including all the Commission's explanatory leaflets.

This leaflet should also be produced in minority ethnic languages, in braille and on tape, so that it is accessible to *all* members of the community. In addition we recommend that the Charity Commission continues to keep under review all its current explanatory leaflets to ensure they are written in as accessible a manner as possible.

The Charity Commission should also issue guidance on the need to check for potential duplication of activities by charities, on appropriate sizes of management committees and on terms of office for trustees as well as on mergers and the winding up of existing charities. The Commission should consult with NCVO and other umbrella bodies before finalising the content of this new guidance.

As well as producing written material, the Charity Commission should be able to provide trustees or their staff with advice. However, there is an important distinction to be made between the general advice on objectives, management, fundraising and constitutional questions which an organisation requires when it is considering becoming a charity and more specific questions which trustees or their staff may wish to put to the Charity Commission regarding some aspect of charity law.

As already indicated, we believe the Charity Commission should continue to participate in other agencies' training events, since its presence lends authority to the proceedings and provides a good opportunity for trustees and their staff to raise issues directly with Commission staff.

Finally, we recommend that the Charity Commission convene a standing committee of relevant organisations with NCVO to ensure the recommendations in this report are implemented.

NATIONAL COUNCIL FOR VOLUNTARY ORGANISATIONS

We believe that there is an urgent need for NCVO to provide a lead within the voluntary sector on the issue of trustee training. We are *not* suggesting that all advice, support and training for trustees should be *provided* by NCVO – that would be neither practicable nor desirable. We *are* suggesting that NCVO, as the main representative body for the voluntary sector in England, should work with other relevant agencies in developing trustee support services and in producing the core material for a trustee handbook, as well as playing a co-ordinating and enabling role in helping new forms of provision to develop.

Since charity trustees and members of voluntary management committees are one of the defining features of the voluntary sector (without them there would literally be no voluntary sector), it is important that NCVO's work addresses their needs and interests. Giving greater priority to working with trustees will involve reviewing mailing lists, the type of information produced and the timing of its meetings. We recommend that NCVO review all its current working arrangements with these considerations in mind. It is particularly important for NCVO to work with the chairs of national charities.

NCVO already performs an advisory role to voluntary organisations through its Legal Department, which handles over 4,000 enquiries a year, and through its other advice teams, including Management Development and Personnel. However, NCVO does not currently have the capacity to help others develop the trustee support services of the kind required. We therefore recommend that NCVO, working with other relevant organisations, establish a development unit for trustee support services, which would

- develop existing advice, support and training through working with other relevant agencies;
- train trainers and other advisers (including professionals such as solicitors) working with trustees;
- advise other providers on content and approach;
- maintain a database of available advice, support and training for trustees;
- publicise sources of advice, support and training for trustees; and
- develop and maintain a network of trustees, particularly focusing on the chairs of charities and voluntary organisations.

The development unit for trustee support services should *not* become directly involved in particular types of provision (although NCVO will doubtless continue to be one of the agencies providing advice to trustees). It should maintain a more strategic role in *developing* provision. The focus of the development unit would be solely on trustees rather than on paid staff.

We suggest that NCVO should convene a steering group with a range of other organisations to help develop trustee advisory services. These should include the Volunteer Centre UK and relevant national networks of local development agencies, through whom many of the services would be delivered. It is also important that trustees themselves are involved in the steering group. Over time, through the network of trustees supported by the development unit, it would be possible to establish a representative management committee of trustees to oversee the development unit and, perhaps, eventually make it a free-standing body.

We also suggest that NCVO should produce the core material for the trustees', handbook referred to in Recommendation 16 and encourage other national networks and charities to add to or adapt it to suit their particular needs. This could also be done with support from the steering group for the development unit.

As indicated above, the Charity Commission should convene a standing committee with NCVO and other relevant organisations to ensure the recommendations in this report are implemented. As part of this process, NCVO should work with others to develop the costings of the proposals in this report and encourage central and local government, the private sector and charitable trusts to invest in them as appropriate. Developing an action plan for implementing the report's recommendations will be an important part of this process.

THE ROLE OF OTHER AGENCIES

As we have emphasised above, there is a wide range of agencies which have an important role to play in the provision of advice, support and training for trustees in addition to the Charity Commission and NCVO.

Within the voluntary sector, development agencies such as the Volunteer Centre UK, the National Association of Councils for Voluntary Service, Action with Communities in Rural England, the National Association of Volunteer Bureaux and the National Federation of Community Organisations all have an important contribution to make – as do their local members. More specialist development agencies such as the Organisation Development Unit for Ethnic Minorities, the National Alliance of Women's Organisations, the Institute of Charity Fundraising Managers, Charity Evaluation Services and other specialist networks can also help provide advice, support and training for trustees within their membership or constituency. National federations also have an important contribution in providing advice, support and training to their local members.

A wide range of other trainers, consultants and companies also have a role in developing and delivering appropriate forms of provision, for example in evaluating performance by financial and non-financial criteria. Professional institutes, such as the Law Society and the Institute of Chartered Accountants, also have opportunities to support and advise their members, many of whom will be one of the main sources of advice for many local charities.

NATIONAL NETWORKS

The kind of training and resource materials which will suit one type or size of organisation will often be inappropriate for another. National networks of voluntary organisations – where a national body is servicing the needs of its own members or branches – are therefore particularly well placed to play a role in trustee training. Indeed it is significant that local surveys of the need for advice, carried out by NCVO, are showing that as many as 70 per cent of local charities and voluntary organisations look to their national body as their main source of advice and support.

How national federations can support their members

A walk down any high street will provide numerous examples of local voluntary organisations affiliated to a parent national body, such as Citizens Advice Bureaux, Help the Aged, Oxfam and MIND. Although they have different aims and objectives, they share a common feature, some would call it constructive tension, which marks the relationship between the national office and the local federated group.

A number of national agencies have sought to influence and persuade their local network of groups to improve the quality of their service and governance. Some now provide induction and refresher training courses for management committee members in their roles and responsibilities on a regional and local level.

Serious efforts are also made to apply, monitor and review standards of provision and good practice in administration and financial control. The main tool used is a manual, prepared after consultation with local representatives. Manuals very enormously, but for the most part cover the following areas:

- history of the organisation;
- legal background;
- principles;
- mission and objectives;
- structure, organisation and respective roles;
- procedure for resolutions, appeals and complaints;
- recognition of membership and use of name or emblem;
- long-term strategy;
- trustees' responsibilities;
- policy on volunteers and friends;
- recruitment, team building, communication and training;
- certificates and awards;
- fundraising code;
- publicity;
- finance and accountability;
- quotas and fees to centre;
- grants from centre;
- insurance, employment, admin systems and computerisation.

An organisational manual is a crucial training tool, particularly for the local Committee of a federated national body. It is often left to the regional association to implement a training programme for the Committees and staff of the local network of groups.

A good example of the way a national network can function is provided by Action with Communities in Rural England (ACRE), the national network of Rural Community Councils (RCCs). ACRE and the RCCs support village halls, of which there are around 8,000 in England, managed by 60–70,000 trustees under a village hall charitable trust deed. Most village halls belong to RCCs and their trustees have access to a county village hall adviser, and to national advice through Village Halls Forum. Many attend conferences, seminars and training days at district or county level. ACRE also provides a good publications service geared specifically to the needs of village halls.

Other national networks of local organisations provide programmes of support for their members – for example the Pre-school Playgroups Association, the National Federation of Women's Institutes, the Association of Independent Museums and many others – but many would acknowledge that they need training themselves in order to provide appropriate support for trustees and all would say they are not adequately funded to do the job properly. Furthermore, many of these national networks are finding it increasingly difficult to maintain their *present* core funding services, since there has been a tendency by Government departments in recent years to favour time-limited project funding at the expense of core funding. Many grants have also failed to keep pace with inflation.

We therefore recommend in Chapter 18 that central and local government, and other funders, recognise the need to invest in the infrastructure needed to provide advice, support and training to local organisations and their trustees, through increased core funding to specific national networks.

LOCAL DEVELOPMENT AGENCIES

Most voluntary action is organised and managed at the local level and although many local groups look to their national body for advice and support, there are a number of local groups which do not have a national body. Furthermore, certain types of training, such as an introduction to the responsibilities of trustees, are often more appropriately done at local level.

Local Development Agencies (LDAs) such as councils for voluntary service, rural community councils and some volunteer bureaux can provide a wide range of support as well as being very effective channels of communication with local groups. Specialist LDAs can either perform a similar function in relation to a particular constituency, such as the role played by Black LDAs in some areas in relation to Black and ethnic minority groups; or can provide a particular type of advice or support, such as community accountancy projects and some law centres.

Courses run by councils for voluntary service

A number of councils for voluntary service are working at a local level to improve the quality and effectiveness of Committees.

Voluntary Action Lewisham secured funding from the Community Development Unit of the local council to hold a one-day Committee training course. The Saturday training day was free to participants with a returnable deposit on completion. The range of topics considered included the purpose and function of community organisations, types of committees and the roles and responsibilities of Committee members. One positive outcome of the course was the sharing of experiences, ideas and concerns with other Committee members from a cross-section of community groups.

Brighton CVS runs a six-week evening class entitled 'The Effective Committee Member'. This gives people an opportunity to put their newly acquired knowledge, skills and expertise into practice and to be able to report back to the group on how they are progressing with their own Committee. Job descriptions for Committee members are explored, their role as an employer and decision-making procedures are among the subjects covered.

Stockport CVS sent out a questionnaire to all CVS in the Greater Manchester area to discover what new developments and support work with Committees were being planned and whether CVS would be willing to share their training, the costs of joint training and the results and benefits of any courses conducted. 'This could be an innovative way of tackling this issue with fresh eyes', according to the CVS Secretary, 'particularly when local CVS can't afford to put on special courses of this nature.'

He is also interested in persuading local TECs to recognise their role in the provision of management training for all staff, paid or unpaid. In this way a new source of support and training could be provided to the army of voluntary management committee members.

All these different kinds of LDAs have a potential role to play in providing advice and support for trustees at a local level. For example, all the training centres in the NCVO Short Course Programme – the largest training programme for local groups in the country – are LDAs. Unfortunately, there are many parts of the country without an LDA of any kind, and, furthermore, many of those that exist are currently experiencing cuts in their local authority funding.

We therefore recommend in Chapter 18 that central and local government, and other funders, recognise the need to invest in LDAs to enable them to develop increased advice, support and training for trustees.

SPECIALIST PROVIDERS OF ADVICE

We have already identified the need for trustees to have access to particular types of advice, including legal and financial advice. Sometimes, this will be available from their own paid staff or from the Charity Commission, NCVO or their national network or local development agency. However, sometimes they will need particular types of specialist advice which may not be available from these sources.

There are, of course, professional firms available to provide this kind of advice on a commercial basis. However, many smaller charities are unable to pay full commercial rates. Furthermore, there is some evidence to suggest that even when they can afford to pay, charities do not always receive a service attuned to their needs. For example, many solicitors are unfamiliar with charity law; many accountants are unfamiliar with the variety of funding relationships between voluntary groups and government agencies. There is therefore a need to develop an increased awareness of the voluntary sector among the professions.

We therefore recommend that NCVO, working with other organisations such as the Action Resource Centre and Business in the Community, explore new ways of increasing awareness of the voluntary sector among professions, as well as building on current initiatives for increasing the provision of free advice.

Lawyers in the Community

Lawyers in the Community is a volunteering scheme organised by Action Resource Centre for qualified solicitors in firms in the City of London and voluntary organisations in four London inner city boroughs. The scheme provides a brokerage service for lawyers who wish to get involved on the management committees of local voluntary organisations working to address the needs the community.

Training sessions begin by clarifying what is understood by the term 'voluntary sector' and how organisations in this category differ from private and public sector organisations. They explore the role of management committees and the roles and responsibilities their members hold. They aim to develop a general understanding of the nature of voluntary groups, their management structure and the kinds of issues that are likely to be tackled at this level.

The volunteers have been useful to their organisations in a number of ways, beyond their specific legal expertise:

- Interviewing candidates for work;
- Employment contracts – terms of employment;
- Redundancy packages;
- Financial management;
- Clarifying relations with the funding body;
- Helping to make the scheme more commercial;
- Private sector financing responsibilities;
- Debit financing;
- Fundraising;
- Helping to draft letters to institutions and charities;
- Dealing with local authorities;
- Ensuring compliance with the constitution;
- Ensuring meetings are structured so as to deal with business efficiently;
- Preparation of minutes and agendas;
- Preparation of policy documents;

- Drafting simple agreements;
- Review of lease;
- Taking up of new lease of premises;
- Incorporation as a company limited by guarantee;
- Giving a commercial view;
- Future directions;

Another type of specialist service which requires developing is advice to the 40,000 village charities in England, with upwards of 140,000 trustees and an annual disbursement of £200 million. These charities suffer from a variety of problems, including lack of any form of established national network, aims which are often out of date, mainly white professional trustees (usually, in effect, life appointments) and ignorance of their responsibilities.

In order to address these problems, we recommend that:

- steps be taken to develop a national network of local charities, including an advice and training programme, through establishing a new agency, initially based at Action with Communities in Rural England, to run and service the network;
- the National Association of Local Councils should encourage local parish councils, which make about 30% of trustee appointments for local charities, to exercise their powers in a responsible and active way to try and widen the range of trustees appointed; and
- the new agency should develop resource materials and training programmes for local charities.

Derbyshire Rural Community Council training initiative

The training needs of trustees in rural areas is often overlooked. The Derbyshire and Leicestershire Rural Community Councils have joined forces to offer an evening seminar for trustees of local charities to begin to address this issue. The tutors tackled a range of topics, including:

- the Charity Commission;
- roles and duties of trustees and clerks;
- updating objects, rationalising small charities, schemes; and
- identifying beneficiaries.

Participants were encouraged to ask questions throughout the seminar and to discuss particular problems and challenges faced by them at a local level. They were provided with an information pack which brought together a range of leaflets and specially prepared material.

The seminar was well received, with an overwhelming demand for further courses, particularly on charity law and the Charity Commission. Weekday evenings were identified as the most popular time for voluntary Committee members.

Derbyshire RCC is now hoping to secure funding for a local charities adviser who will produce an information pack for trustees which can be bought by local groups and plan more specialist courses for small rural charities in the area.

TRAINERS AND CONSULTANTS

The effectiveness of training and other support depends on the competence of consultants, trainers and other advisers. We received evidence from a number of consultants and trainers, who demonstrated wide knowledge, experience and insight into the issues facing trustees and Committees.

We expect national and local development agencies for the voluntary sector to extend the brokerage they currently provide in order to ensure that the trustees of charities have access to competent consultants and trainers.

We envisage that the publication of our report and growing interest in the issue of trustee training will result in an expansion of the number of trainers and consultants operating in this field. It is clearly important they recognise the differing needs of trustees in different types of organisation.

Clearly, a major factor affecting the role of trainers and consultants will be whether or not charities and voluntary organisations have the resources to purchase their services. We address this issue in Chapter 18.

We recommend that our report is widely promoted to trainers and consultants to ensure that they take on board our suggestions. We also recommend that the new development unit for trustee support services works with trainers and consultants on these issues.

EDUCATIONAL INSTITUTIONS

We have already welcomed the development of distance learning for members of voluntary Committees. There is clearly considerable scope for the Open University to develop further initiatives in this field.

More generally, colleges of higher and further education and adult education agencies such as the Workers' Education Association should review the scope for developing courses for trustees. We recommend that they discuss possible initiatives with councils for voluntary service and rural community councils in their areas. Some LDAs have already developed effective collaboration with colleges – for example some of the local projects in the Advancing Good Management Scheme, supported from NCVO.

CENTRAL GOVERNMENT

We discuss the role of central government as a funder in Chapter 18. In this chapter, we are more concerned with central government as a potential provider of advice, support and training for trustees and as a potential source of trustees.

As a general rule, we think it is preferable for training to be provided independently of funders such as central government. We would, however, expect any funder to provide advice to trustees when they request it or at least to point them in the direction of suitable sources. There is also scope for creating more opportunities for civil servants and trustees to learn about each others' roles, perhaps through offering places on Civil Service College courses, to some trustees or arranging seminars and workshops on issues of common concern.

The civil service is also a major potential source of trustees. We therefore recommend that the government takes positive steps to encourage civil servants to become trustees, including arranging opportunities for them to be briefed about the role and responsibilities of trustees, circulating details about charities who are seeking additional trustees (perhaps through the Trustees Register) and introducing a paid leave scheme for trustees, perhaps along the lines of the British Gas, Esso and IBM schemes for school governors. However, we do not recommend that government departments nominate civil servants to be trustees for organisations they fund.

LOCAL GOVERNMENT

Local government plays a much larger role than central government as a direct provider of advice to charities and voluntary organisations. Officers in legal, finance and development departments frequently provide technical advice to voluntary organisations in their areas.

As indicated above, we think this advice is better provided independently, especially as funding relationships become more contractual. In any event, the introduction of compulsory competitive tendering and internal service agreements into these areas is beginning to reduce the availability of this free advice. Local authorities should, therefore, concentrate on helping independent sources of advice develop for the voluntary sector.

Local authority members and officers are often trustees of organisations funded by the councils on which they serve. This situation can often create a conflict of interest since, as a trustee, the person's only concern must be the charity, whereas, as a member or officer, the person has a duty to protect the interests of the funder. For this reason it may often be better for members and officers to be non-voting observers, rather than trustees as such. This issue is beyond the remit of our report and is not covered in our recommendations.

Where there is no conflict of interest involved, there is scope for encouraging more local authority officers to become trustees in their personal capacity in just the same way as we have recommended for civil servants. There is also scope for opening up some of the training provided for local authority members to charity trustees. We feel each could learn from the other. This could apply at the individual authority level and also in relation to initiatives promoted by the local authority associations and the Local Government Management Board.

THE PRIVATE SECTOR

The private sector has an important role to play in encouraging people to become trustees and providing them with the training required to take on the role. Bodies such as the Institute of Directors could encourage their members in this way. Professional institutes such as the Institute of Chartered Accountants, British Institute of Management and the Association of Management Consultants could all increase their members' awareness of the role of charity trustees.

More generally, the Action Resource Centre (ARC) plays an important role in promoting secondment from the private to the voluntary sector. At present, their work focuses on secondment to paid posts. However, we recommend that ARC explores the scope for initiatives to encourage more private sector employees to be seconded to voluntary organisations as trustees. ARC could usefully work with Business in the Community and the Trustees Register on this.

A number of private companies already allow voluntary sector employees access to their training courses. We recommend this is also extended to trustees. There would be particular value in allowing them access to training provided for non-executive directors.

Employee volunteering

Many voluntary organisations complain that they cannot attract enough people of the right calibre and range of experience onto their Committees. Increasingly, groups are looking to the private sector to recruit potential trustees. The Volunteer Centre UK has explored the emerging company-owned employee volunteering schemes.

Two ways in which a company can support employee involvement is by helping to establish and provide support for staff charity Committees or fundraising teams. A firm can also recruit and place new volunteers by compiling a list of staff willing to serve as members of a Committee of community groups and matching them with requests. These are known as management committee banks.

The Body Shop recently took top honours in the UK Awards for Employee Volunteering. Each staff member of the Body Shop is allowed a half-day's paid leave a month for voluntary activity. New staff must perform at least one day's voluntary work in the first six months with the company.

Schemes such as this are increasing the numbers of skilled volunteers while the employers are gaining from an improved image in the local community and the use of voluntary work as a staff development tool.

IBM's Edinburgh office received an award for their imaginative Local Environmental Action Teams (LEAT) programme and the way they have harnessed employee volunteering to local environmental groups on practical projects. Attention was paid to ensuring that the activities led to benefits for the volunteers and that the transfer was not all one way.

The LEAT programme's aim was to help in cash grants and in people giving 'IBM added-value' in terms of skills and equipment. Data-bases of environmental groups were established and management training seminars for environmental groups set up as part of a wider package of projects and tasks.

SUMMARY

In this chapter, we have considered what action could be taken by a range of different agencies to improve the advice, support and training available to trustees.

We have highlighted the role of the Charity Commission and NCVO but we have also stressed that the delivery of advice, support and training must come from a wide range of other agencies.

RECOMMENDATIONS

18 The Charity Commission should produce a new basic leaflet aimed at potential and existing trustees outlining in very clear, simple terms their responsibilities and roles. This leaflet should aim to provide all potential and existing trustees with essential introductory information, from which they could then go on to look at the range of existing booklets already available from the Charity Commission.

19 The leaflet should be sent to all charities with the new annual charity return in sufficient quantities for each trustee to have one. The Charity Commission should also send it to any new or potential trustees who come to its notice and copies should be available at other outlets, such as local libraries, local development agencies and citizen advice bureaux. It should also be sent to organisations which supply large numbers of trustees such as local authorities and companies, and be produced in minority ethnic languages, in braille and on tape.

20 The Charity Commission should continue to keep under review all its current explanatory leaflets to ensure that they are written in as accessible a manner as possible, and expand its range of advice by issuing guidance on:

- the potential duplication of activities between charities;
- appropriate sizes of Committees;
- terms of office for trustees;
- mergers of existing charities; and
- the winding up of charities.

The Charity Commission should consult with NCVO and other umbrella bodies before finalising the content of this new guidance.

21 The Charity Commission should play a leading role within government in trying to persuade government, local authorities and other funders to invest in improving provision of advice, support and training for trustees.

22 The Charity Commission should convene a standing committee of relevant organisations with NCVO to review the provision of advice, support and training for trustees on an ongoing basis.

23 NCVO should give much higher priority to working with trustees and particularly their chairs, than it has done hitherto and should take steps to ensure that its work and services are accessible to them. This will have implications for its mailing lists, the type of information it produces and the timing of meetings it organises.

24 NCVO, working with relevant organisations, should establish a development unit for trustee support services which would:

- develop existing advice, support and training, through working with other relevant agencies;
- train trainers and other advisers (including professionals such as solicitors) working with trustees;
- advise other providers on content and approach;
- maintain a database of available advice, support and training for trustees;
- publicise sources of advice, support and training for trustees;
- develop and maintain a network of trustees, particularly focusing on the chairs of charities and of voluntary organisations.

The development unit should maintain a more strategic role in developing provision.

25 NCVO should produce the core material for the information pack referred to in Recommendation 8 and encourage other national networks and charities to add to or adapt it to suit their particular needs.

26 Generalist and specialist development agencies, federations and networks within the voluntary sector, nationally and locally, should consider how they can best contribute to the provision of advice, support and training for trustees. They should draw on the expertise of consultants and trainers with experience of meeting the needs of trustees. Particular consideration should be given to the need for advice and support to the 40,000 rural grant-giving charities in England.

27 Action Resource Centre and Business in the Community should explore ways of increasing awareness of the voluntary sector among the professions, as well as building on current initiatives for increasing free advice provision.

28 Colleges of further and higher education, education agencies and youth and community organisations should discuss possible initiatives for training trustees with local development agencies such as Councils for Voluntary Service and Rural Community Councils.

29 Other agencies, such as local authorities and companies, should consider whether any of the training they provide for local authority councillors and non-executive directors could, appropriately, be made available to trustees. They should also consider providing those of their own staff who wish to become trustees with appropriate training.

18 Action by government and other funders

INTRODUCTION

One of the most common remarks made to the Working Party was the need for increased investment in trustee training if anything concrete were to result from the Working Party's efforts. We agree with this view and would point to the investment which *has* taken place recently, for example, in school governor training and in support for small businesses.

Charities struggling to raise money for their core expenditure are unlikely to spend resources on training for trustees. Generalist and specialist development agencies will need resources to develop the range of provision we have recommended.

Although we accept that resources in themselves will not result in the improvements we are seeking, we do stress there must be more money available. We also believe that *all* funders have a responsibility to contribute towards this investment.

We are encouraged by the fact that a number of government, private sector and charitable funders have said they will await the Working Party's report before making decisions about what initiatives to support in this field. The Prime Minister's explicit reference to the Working Party in his speech at the November 1991 Charities Aid Foundation Conference was also encouraging.

In this chapter, therefore, we consider what action is required by government and other funders, not only in terms of specific financial help but also in terms of their funding relationships with charities and voluntary organisations.

INVESTMENT REQUIRED

We recommend that the Voluntary Services Unit in the Home Office take a lead role in central government in helping to implement the recommendations in this report and in ensuring a co-ordinated response, including a funding contribution, from central government to the recommendations in this report.

We would also recommend that funders, particularly those who take a medium or long-term view, including central and local government, trusts and private companies, should recognise the importance of promoting trustee training and should respond positively to initiatives for increasing the effectiveness of trustees. We believe that investment of this kind will in turn increase the effectiveness of funders' own programmes. Bodies such as the Association of Charitable Foundations, the local authority associations, Business in the Community and the Charities Aid Foundation can all help reinforce this message. At the same time, those wishing to promote trustee training must come forward with initiatives; many funders informed us that they had never actually been asked to fund trustee training.

Three forms of investment are required. First, direct funding is needed for some of the initiatives recommended in this report. Secondly, core funding is needed for national networks and local development agencies to enable them to provide advice, support and training to their members' trustees. Thirdly, all voluntary organisations need to be able to afford to pay for training for their trustees. Each of these is discussed below.

Direct investment is particularly required for the following initiatives:

- Charity Commission leaflets (see Recommendations 18, 19, 20);
- Core handbook for trustees (see Recommendations 8, 25);
- Development unit for trustee advisory services (see Recommendations 9 and 24); and
- Distance learning initiatives (see Recommendation 7).

We also recommend that core funding is increased for national networks and local development agencies to provide them with the capacity to promote good practice, ensure high standards and provide effective training, advice and support at accessible prices. We are not able to provide an estimate of the cost implications at this stage, but we recommend that NCVO works with these other agencies to identify them.

Finally, we recommend that grants and contracts with individual charities and voluntary organisations allow for expenditure on trustee training as a legitimate item. This will enable them to purchase advice, support and training for their trustees and thus encourage appropriate forms of supply to develop. Funders should encourage applicants to allow for this expenditure in their budget estimates. In some situations, it may be appropriate for a funder to maintain a central budget for trustee training and fund training activities for all the organisations it funds directly from this budget. This could be more cost effective as far as a local funder is concerned and would have the added advantage of not increasing the administrative overheads of individual charities.

FUNDING RELATIONSHIPS

As well as providing resources, funders are well placed to influence the organisations they fund, either directly through funding conditions or, more indirectly, through the relationships they develop with applicants and funded organisations. The recent Efficiency Scrutiny Review into the funding of voluntary organisations by central government recognised the importance of increasing the effectiveness of these funding relationships.

However, it has to be recognised that giving greater priority to developing effective funding relationships also requires additional investment. Funders themselves will need the appropriate staff and expertise.

Virtually all funders communicate with organisations' paid staff rather than with their trustees. And yet, it is the trustees who are legally responsible for ensuring that the funding conditions are met and that the organisation is fully accountable and effective. We therefore recommend that funders should ask for details of the trustees of the organisations that they fund. In suitable cases they should meet with the trustees to help ensure that the voluntary organisations they fund are effectively managed.

Good practice by funders

A number of grant-giving trusts are developing positive ways to support trustees in their work. The Consortium on Opportunities for Volunteering feels it is crucial that management committees have an understanding of their role. They have now introduced a compulsory training session for at least two Committee members before the grant period is to begin. This requirement is spelt out in the grant application pack.

The one-day event seeks to explain what the Consortium expects of organisations and their trustees and what they can expect of the Consortium. The information-sharing sessions cover the financial reporting procedures they will have to adhere to over the coming three years. Also, how to develop an equal opportunities policy for all aspects of the organisation, including recruitment of staff, and the basics of evaluation and monitoring techniques are discussed and guidance given on the relevant information and statistics they will need to collect.

The Consortium's co-ordinator feels Committee members must realise their responsibilities and not just leave it to paid members of staff and that they must come to recognise the need for staff training, particularly in small organisations. The Consortium will also provide funds (usually 5 per cent of the total grant amount) for further training in years two and three. This may be provided in-house or from outside agencies. She feels that this is the best way to provide support for groups and their Committees.

Funders may sometimes wish to indicate an element in a grant for training trustees, particularly when Committees are inexperienced. The Department of Health's funding scheme, the Consortium on Opportunities for Volunteering, based at the Volunteer Centre UK, requires all successful grant applicants to attend training courses before they are given any grant. Equal opportunities and staff recruitment are major themes in the training provided.

Increasingly, funders are establishing mechanisms for monitoring and evaluating the progress of the organisations they fund in relation to their objectives. If done on an agreed basis, with the recipient of grant, this is possible even for charitable trusts with few, if any, paid staff. It would then highlight situations where additional advice or support may be required, including training of trustees.

Trust for London

The Trust for London, set up after the abolition of the GLC, has developed evaluation and monitoring processes for all their grant-aided groups. All organisations are sent a form after the money has been used and they are asked various financial and descriptive questions. The Clerk to the Trustees explains: 'We wish to know if they have achieved what they set out to do. Have they met their objectives? We also like to know if other monies have been generated as a result of the Trust for London grant.'

Many groups funded by the Trust have also had a monitoring visit to discuss at greater length the issues they faced and to help the Trust develop its own policies. An exercise has been completed on the first 500 groups funded, all refugee groups and community transport groups which have received support. The Clerk says:

We have learned that groups welcome the monitoring visits and the opportunity to discuss the pressures they are under to provide their service. We've also learnt that monitoring takes much more time than expected. In my opinion, it is only useful if the results of the evaluation changes our own grant-making policies. Groups often need more help than just money.

Funders may also want to monitor the turnover of trustees. In particular circumstances, a funder may wish to make suggestions about the composition of the Committee – for example, the inclusion of an accountant or a business person.

Generally funders should be aware of the range of different forms of advice, support and training available for trustees, so they can advise the organisations they fund where to go for help. The most effective way of doing this will be through funders maintaining links with the development unit for trustee support services, which will maintain a database of provision and perform a signposting role.

SUMMARY

In this chapter we have considered what action is required by government and other funders not only in terms of investment, but also in terms of their funding relationships generally with charities and voluntary organisations.

We recognise that for many funders the recommendations may be ideals to work towards, rather than practices which can be implemented immediately. We make no apologies for this, but would urge all funders to try and move in the direction we are suggesting.

RECOMMENDATIONS

Investment

30 Funders should increase their investment in the provision of advice, support and training for trustees. Grants and contracts with individual charities and voluntary organisations should allow for expenditure on trustee training.

31 The Voluntary Services Unit in the Home Office should take a lead role in central government in helping to implement the recommendations of this report and in ensuring a co-ordinated response, including a funding contribution from central government, to the recommendations in this report.

32 Core funding should be increased for national and local development agencies and networks to enable them to develop their provision of trustee training.

Funding relationships

33 Funders should ask for details of trustees and try to meet with some of them, as well as with the paid staff. This may often involve funders having to arrange meetings outside normal office hours.

34 Funders should encourage all trustees to think about their training needs. When providing funding, funders should, where appropriate, separately identify an element for staff and trustee training, and advise the organisations they fund on appropriate sources of advice, support and training for trustees.

35 Funders should, as far as possible, establish mechanisms for monitoring and evaluating the governance of the organisations they fund and, where necessary, require additional trustee training to take place.

19 Action by individual trustees

INTRODUCTION

Although individual charities, their paid staff and national and local agencies all have very important roles to play in helping to increase the effectiveness of trustees, ultimately it is trustees themselves who are responsible for the overall governance of their organisation – and it is trustees themselves who must ensure that they get the right advice, support and training.

There are a number of ways in which trustees can contribute to their own effectiveness at an individual level. We have identified four important dimensions:

- deciding whether to become a trustee;
- performing effectively as a trustee;
- taking on responsibilities; and
- knowing when to resign.

In this chapter we also discuss the proposal to establish an association of trustees.

DECIDING WHETHER TO BECOME A TRUSTEE

A person may be invited to become a trustee, may be nominated or elected or may volunteer their services – for example, by registering with the Trustee Register. Whatever route is taken, the first responsibility is to find out about the roles and responsibilities of trustees generally and to get a clear idea what the particular organisation expects.

In future, potential trustees should ask their charity to provide them with the leaflet we have recommended that the Charity Commission produce setting out what is involved in becoming a trustee. They should also ask for a statement of what is expected of them, including a job description and a person specification where they exist, and a copy of the charity's constitution and annual report and accounts.

The principles which apply to good staff recruitment practice apply equally to trustee recruitment. The organisation should spell out what it expects the trustee to do, what kind of person it is looking for and how much time is likely to be involved. If a potential trustee is not given this information, he or she should ask for it.

In the light of this information, potential trustees must then decide whether they have the right skills and experience to do the job and whether they can commit the time involved. Part of their assessment may well depend on the amount of advice, support and training which is going to be made available.

Those thinking of becoming trustees – or approaching others to become trustees – should assess how far they are likely to demonstrate the following:

1 *Commitment to the mission of the organisation.* Unless that commitment is there at the outset, it is very unlikely the trustee will be prepared to carry out his or her responsibilities effectively.
2 *Commitment of time.* A Charity Recruitment survey in 1989 found that many of those who serve as trustees also work full time or have other commitments. Nonetheless 46 per cent gave more than 20 hours a month to their work with the charity; 29 per cent gave more than 30 hours a month. Potential trustees must assess whether they can commit the time required.
3 *Judgement.* As trustees, they will be required to make important decisions affecting the future of the organisation – to appoint staff, decide on fundraising initiatives, take risks. This all involves judgement.
4 *Strategic vision.* Trustees must be able to consider the longer term and decide where the organisation is going. Where there are paid staff, trustees can have the advantage of being able to step back and take a wider view. Where there are no paid staff, trustees must still have a strategic vision, as well as being able to handle day-to-day business. They must also have the confidence and courage to act on this strategic vision.
5 *Leadership potential.* Trustees, especially the honorary officers, will often need to provide foresight and leadership to the organisation – both to staff (where they exist) and to the organisation's supporters. New trustees may also be future honorary officers.
6 *Discretion in working with others.* Trustees will often be considering confidential matters relating to the staffing, funding or future direction of the organisation. They will also often find themselves wearing two hats – for example as an employee of one

voluntary organisation and a trustee of another. Discretion in these situations is vital.

7 *Ability to work in a team.* There will normally be at least three trustees – often many more. The experience and background of the other trustees will often be very varied; some may be users, others may be workers in other voluntary organisations, others may be from the private or public sectors. Being able to work together as a team is therefore very important.

8 *Understanding of the voluntary sector.* There is no point in having all the attributes described above if, at the same time, the person has no understanding of the concept of a voluntary Committee or of the significance of involving and supporting volunteers. Trustees also need to appreciate the ways in which voluntary organisations are often accountable to a wide range of interest groups, including funders and users, as well as being aware of the realities of fundraising and grant-aid. They also need to be aware of the wider voluntary sector.

Some trustees will have these attributes at the outset. Others will need to develop them through experience. What is important is that both the organisation and the trustee recognise the need for these attributes – both when recruiting trustees and when considering their advice, support and training needs.

Competency areas for trustees

The Association of Community Trusts and Foundations has identified seven 'competency areas': community leadership, fundraising, governance, grant giving, investment management and public relations. The checklist looks at competence from the viewpoint of individual trustees or staff members. It can be used to help clarify who should be responsible for what, or to help you prioritise training and information needs. Examples in relation to governance, leadership and fundraising are given below:

Governance

Do you (or should you):

- know what makes community trusts different from other charitable organisations
- know the mission of your trust
- understand the constitution of your trust
- know what formal documents comprise the constitution
- know the areas and programmes within which your trust works
- know the board's government and management structure
- know the board's procedures
- know the criteria for recruitment of board members

- know how to develop/operate in an anti-discriminatory way

Leadership

- understand the role of trustees in providing community leadership
- establish/implement role(s) for the trust as community leaders
- publicise and seek support for unmet community needs

Fundraising

- know the basic motivation for giving
- know different types of gift
- develop/implement the fundraising strategy
- know/identify potential donors
- identify/know donor services provided by the trust
- know donors' requirements
- reconcile donors' wishes with the trust's values and policies

There is clearly a balance to be struck at this stage in the recruitment process between spelling things out in such detail that potential trustees are put off at the outset and misleading people as to what they may be letting themselves in for. It is important to get this balance right and to emphasise the satisfaction and fulfilment to be gained from being a trustee, as well as indicating the responsibilities and work involved.

PERFORMING EFFECTIVELY AS A TRUSTEE

Having decided to become a trustee, there are a number of steps which a person can take to increase his/her effectiveness. In an ideal world, many of the practices recommended below should happen as a matter of course. However, from our survey and the evidence we have received, it is clear the majority of trustees do not function in an ideal world.

Induction for new trustees is essential and is clearly the responsibility of the organisation. However, if a new trustee finds that no such induction has been arranged, he or she should insist it is provided.

Once a trustee has been given a briefing and provided with relevant background information and papers, some organisations, such as Barnardo's, require them to sign a form to confirm they are fully aware of what they have taken on. This is a useful way of signifying that both parties – the organisation and the trustee – have completed the induction process.

Committee meetings

It is helpful to distinguish between trustees' performance at Committee meetings and their performance elsewhere. An important point to emphasise to new trustees is that their involvement with the organisation is expected to be more than simply attending a set number of Committee meetings each year.

Nevertheless, Committee meetings are one of the main arenas for trustees and it is worth stating some basic points about these meetings:

- Trustees should ensure that they are sent Committee papers well in advance of the meeting.
- They should read the papers and identify important issues for discussion or comment.
- They should not be afraid to ask questions and press for reasons for the answers given.
- They should draw on their own expertise, where it is relevant (a common observation is that too many trustees, who may be professionals or business people in their working life, leave their expertise behind once they attend a Committee meeting).
- They should allow others to contribute.

Asking the right questions is one of the most important functions of a trustee. Knowing what to look for in a budget or in a business plan is partly a matter of experience, but also partly a skill which can be taught or developed over time. Simulation exercises are often a good way of developing this skill. For example, induction courses for local authority councillors have included role-playing exercises in which councillors had to question officers about their budget estimates. ('What does central services cover?', 'What allowance has been made for staff vacancies?', 'What would happen if . . .?' are typical questions to consider.)

Relationships with staff

As indicated above, the Committee meetings should not be the only area for the trustee. Where organisations employ staff, trustees should ensure that they have opportunities to meet and support staff, for example through visiting the office and attending staff parties. They can have a very positive impact on staff morale. Trustees are also ambassadors for the organisation and should therefore take every opportunity to promote and publicise its work. Fundraising is another particularly important area of activity.

Through their involvement in Committee meetings or other activities, trustees may sometimes become worried about a particular aspect of the organisation. It is essential that they take action rather than simply keeping the concern to themselves. It may simply be a matter of discussing the issue with the senior staff member, the chair or one of the other members of the Committee or sub-committee. Sometimes it may be necessary to seek independent advice. In other situations it may be appropriate to express the concern publicly at a Committee meeting. The important point is to take some action to address the concern rather than doing nothing. It has been observed that too many trustees have a tendency to behave like 'stunned rabbits' rather than taking an active part in discussion.

Where there are paid staff, the biggest source of tension between them and trustees is probably the division of responsibilities. This particularly applies to the relationship between the chair and the senior staff member. It is a tension which is familiar in other fields such as local government. Part of the difficulty is that the traditional distinction between policy and administration or between strategic decision-making and day-to-day management is not one which can always be made clearly in practice. It is therefore much more important to develop a sense of mutual trust and partnership than to attempt to delineate precisely who should do what. The responsibility of trustees, particularly the chair and honorary officers, must be first to try to foster this partnership and then to identify the most important issues for the trustees to be involved in, but as far as possible to allow staff the freedom to get on with their job.

Because charities and voluntary organisations are, by definition, started, and subsequently run, by one or more committed individuals, there is considerable scope for tensions to develop both with the paid staff and with other trustees who become involved at a later date. The 'founder', who cannot recognise the need for change or who refuses to allow a newly appointed member of staff to get on with their job, is a very familiar phenomenon in the voluntary sector. All trustees must be on the look-out for these situations and endeavour to respond to them sensitively.

Trustees, like everyone else, should evaluate their own effectiveness. A useful approach is a self-audit or questionnaire in which trustees can ask themselves about their own personal effectiveness and that of the organisation. They should then discuss the results with the chair.

Finally, trustees should be aware of their own short-comings and recognise their own need for advice, support and training. It is sometimes argued that professionals and people from the business world do not need any training to be effective trustees, because they know it all already. We emphatically reject this point of view. Everyone will bring some skills and expertise to the role of being a trustee, but equally, everyone will lack some perspective or insight, skills and expertise.

TAKING ON RESPONSIBILITIES

Above all, trustees must ensure that they are aware of the responsibilities they are taking on. Although they may delegate the work involved in these responsibilities to paid staff, they cannot delegate or abrogate the responsibilities themselves. In particular, trustees should ensure that they discharge their responsibilities in terms of their

- legal responsibilities to see that the charity is abiding by its objects and constitution and operating within the constraints of law;
- financial responsibilities to see that any monies and property are held in trust for the beneficiaries of the charity and that all financial matters are properly and effectively managed; and
- managerial responsibilities, including the appointment of, and contractual relationships with, staff (including volunteers); ensuring accountability to funders, users and members; representing the views of the organisation; and strategic planning, including the identification of the mission of the organisation, maintainence of values and evaluation of the organisation's activities.

Honorary officers should ensure that they act as an effective link between the staff and the Committee. They should also provide leadership to the Committee. The roles of the chair and the treasurer are particularly important. See specimen job descriptions given below.

Job description for chair of a Committee

Role

1 as chair, ensure that the Committee fulfils its responsibilities for the governance of the organisation;
2 be a partner to the chief executive, helping him/her achieve the mission of the organisation; and
3 optimise the relationship between the Committee and staff/volunteers.

Responsibilities

1 chair meetings of the Committee; see that it functions effectively, relates well with the staff and fulfils all its duties; with the chief executive, develop agendas for meetings;
2 with the chief executive, recommend composition of the Committee; recommend future chairs with a view to succession;
3 assist the chief executive in recruiting Committee members and other expertise for whatever volunteer members are needed;
4 reflect any concerns staff have in regard to the role of the committee or individual Committee members; relate the concerns of the Committee and other constituencies to the chief executive;
5 present to the Committee an evaluation of the pace, direction and organisational strength of the project;
6 prepare a review of the chief executive and recommend salary for consideration by the appropriate Committee;
7 annually ensure the Committee reviews its structure, role and relationship to staff; be assured the Committee is satisfied and has fulfilled all its responsibilities;
8 act as an additional set of eyes and ears;
9 serve as an alternative spokesperson; and
10 fulfil such other assignments as the chair or chief executive agree are appropriate and desirable for the chair to perform.

The chair should have overall responsibility for ensuring the Committee works well, providing leadership and identifying the need for advice, support or training for Committee members.

The treasurer should have technical expertise appropriate to the scope of the organisation, and should be able to make judgements about the degree of potential risk in a decision (a skill acquired through experience as well as training).

Job description for a treasurer

Role

1 to be assured the organisation remains financially viable and operates proper accounting and reporting procedures; and
2 to be a partner with the chief executive to ensure the future financial stability and prospects for the organisation.

Responsibilities

1 to oversee, approve and present all yearly budgets, quarterly and annual accounts and other relevant financial statements;

2 assist in the formation of the annual balance sheet, income and expenditure accounts and background notes to the accounts;

3 be assured that the accounts are audited (where applicable) in an approved form, included in the annual report and submitted to the relevant statutory bodies;

4 make a formal presentation of the accounts at the AGM and draw attention to important points in a coherent and easily understandable way;

5 be assured that the financial resources of the organisation meet its present and future needs;

6 advise the organisation of the financial implications of any forward plan;

7 help in the formation of a fundraising strategy and, if required, become involved in steering a fundraising campaign;

8 act as a signatory on all bank accounts, loans, investments and other financial documents;

9 be assured the investment policy of the organisation is both competitive and ethical in line with the organisation's mission; and

10 ensure the committee is aware of all their financial duties and liabilities in the exercise of their responsibilities.

KNOWING WHEN TO RESIGN

A Charity Recruitment questionnaire in 1989 on trusteeship in the voluntary sector concluded that a small group of committed individuals is providing the backbone of voluntary leadership.

People are often unable to maintain the commitment required to be a trustee. One trustee described the life cycle of trustees as follows:

- start as an energetic ignoramus;
- make every possible mistake for five years;
- leave as an exhausted expert.

This sentiment demonstrates all too well the commitment, demands and responsibilities on trustees of charities.

It is important, therefore, that trustees know when it is time to retire and when some new blood may be required. We recommend that trustees should be encouraged to consider at least once a year whether they should continue bearing in mind the roles and responsibilities required of them.

AN ASSOCIATION OF TRUSTEES?

We understand proposals are currently being developed for an Association of Charity Trustees. An Association could perform a number of different functions,

including to develop a system of accreditation for trustees, by establishing a code of conduct which all trustees would adhere to.

As already indicated in Chapter 11, a National Center for Non-profit Boards was established in the US in 1988. The Center performs three main functions: it helps individual charities develop trustee training tailored for their needs, it provides a nationwide enquiry service and it promotes and develops resource materials. It does not perform any kind of accreditation role for trustees but it does recommend particular types of resource materials and training as being more or less appropriate.

The advantage of an independent Association for Trustees is that it would provide a focus for trustees (as opposed to paid staff) which is currently completely lacking. On the other hand, given the wide diversity of the voluntary sector, there is a danger that its introduction at the present time could result in an elitist organisation likely to appeal only to the trustees of larger or more traditional charities.

We encountered little support for the idea of an Association for Trustees – either in our survey or in our consultative meeting. There was however strong support for developing trustee support services.

SUMMARY

In this chapter, we have discussed the range of actions which individual trustees can themselves take to increase their effectiveness. We have identified four important dimensions:

- deciding whether to become a trustee;
- performing effectively as a trustee;
- taking on responsibilities; and
- knowing when to resign.

We believe it is very important that both potential and actual trustees give serious consideration to each of these dimensions.

We have not recommended establishing an Association for Trustees in the short term, but feel this proposal might be appropriate at a later date after a trustee network and trustee support services have been developed.

RECOMMENDATIONS

36 All potential trustees should ask their charity to provide them with relevant Charity Commission guidance, including the proposed leaflet (see

Recommendation 18) and a statement of what is expected of them, including a job description and person specification where they exist, and a copy of the charity's constitution and annual report and accounts.

37 All potential trustees should make a careful assessment of the responsibilities involved in being a trustee, including the commitment of time, beyond what may be needed for attendance at meetings.

38 Trustees should ask for appropriate information to be provided by the organisation, and need to

- ensure that they receive relevant papers;
- take appropriate action when they have concerns about the organisation; and
- voice their concerns to the chair or at Committee, and if necessary make contact with the relevant trustee support services (see Recommendations 24 and 26).

39 Trustees agree to undertake, by signing a statement, that they will discharge their legal, financial and managerial responsibilities. Individual trustees should be encouraged to consider at least once a year whether they are willing to continue as a trustee, bearing in mind the roles and responsibilities required of them.

40 The chair should have overall responsibility for exercising leadership and ensuring that the Committee functions effectively and for identifying the need for advice, support or training for Committee members.

20 Conclusion

FURTHER WORK REQUIRED

Inevitably an exercise such as ours identifies issues requiring further work. We have not had time to explore some of these in sufficient depth to make recommendations; others are outside our terms of reference, though very relevant to the objective of increasing the effectiveness of trustees.

In particular, we wish to highlight the following areas for further work.

Increasing the representativeness of trustees

Trustees are not currently representative of society as a whole. We believe steps should be taken to redress this, so that a wider range of people can both contribute to, and benefit from, the experience of being involved in, the voluntary sector.

Provision of adequate advice, support and training is part of what is required. But a number of other measures also need to be examined, such as further emphasis on the voluntary sector in school-teaching and school projects; paid leave or time-off in lieu for employees; implementation of equal opportunity policies; enhanced status for trustees, perhaps through greater use of awards systems, including the honours system; inclusion of a question about trusteeship in the census; secondment of private sector employees to voluntary organisations as trustees; statutory protection under employment law for employees wanting to be trustees (on a par with magistrates and local and health authority members).

Federations

There is a need to consider what support should be given to federations and associations of autonomous local members, so that agreed national policies, standards and best practice are fully observed.

The European dimension

Both the policy and legislative frameworks within which charities function, and the work they undertake, will be increasingly influenced by developments in Europe. There will also be much that charities (and their trustees) in different parts of Europe can learn from each other. The proposed development unit for trustee support services has a crucial role in monitoring these developments and keeping trustees informed. This is a dimension the Working Party thinks should be seriously considered in future years.

Further research

Very little research into the characteristics, needs and perceptions of trustees has been undertaken. And yet trustees are in many ways the most important part of the voluntary sector. A better knowledge of trustees is essential if appropriate, relevant materials and training are to be developed. There is no substitute for proper, ongoing research to take the guesswork out of such development.

IMPLEMENTATION AND ACTION PLAN

We are very conscious that a report such as ours could end up sitting on desks or shelves without any action taking place. We are determined this should not happen.

Recommendation 22 is that the Charity Commission should convene a standing committee of relevant organisations with NCVO to review the provision of advice, support and training for trustees on an ongoing basis. As a first step, we envisage that this committee will approach all the agencies identified in our report and ask them to respond to our recommendations within six months, stating clearly what action they intend to take. The committee will then monitor progress against their responses and thus ensure that our recommendations are carried forward.

We wish to emphasise the need for immediate action to implement our recommendations on:

- ensuring that charities help their trustees by telling them what is expected of them and giving them the information they need about their organisation, with effective induction procedures and continuing support;
- giving trustees information and advice, including new leaflet from the Charity Commission; and
- encouraging providers of management training to make their courses and materials as accessible to trustees as they are to staff;
- ensuring that NCVO establishes a development unit to work with a wide range of national and local agencies to develop trustee advisory services for all kinds of voluntary organisations; and
- increasing the resources for developing advice and support services for trustees, from central as local government, trusts and the private sector.

We recognise that some recommendations will require a longer timescale to implement, but the standing committee will be discussing implementation arrangements with all those involved. In this way we aim to make the proper support of trustees a reality for the hundreds of thousands of active citizens running charities and voluntary organisations in England.

Glossary

In this report, we have been aware that it is important to be clear about what we mean when we talk of trustees, committees, and so on, with reference to different kinds and sizes of organisation in the voluntary sector. We hope this short glosssary will be helpful to the reader.

Charities and voluntary organisations

A *registered charity* is a voluntary organisation registered with the Charity Commission. It has a charity number.

A *voluntary organisation* may or may not be a charity. It is managed overall by a voluntary body, known as a board or management committee, or some similar title, which has ultimate legal responsibility for its activities. A voluntary organisation may be charitable, even if unregistered, if it has charitable objects. A charity may be incorporated, i.e. registered as a charitable company limited by guarantee, in which case the trustees are also directors of the company.

An *exempt* or *excepted charity* is a charity which is not required to register with the Charity Commission.

Staffing

Different organisations have *chief executives, directors, general secretaries, co-ordinators*, and so on. In general, we refer to them as *senior staff members.*

Many voluntary organisations, including community organisations and selp-help groups as well as small fundgiving trusts, have no paid staff, and those who have overall responsibility for their activities may be the same people who carry them out. We therefore refer to staff as those carrying out day-to-day activities including management whether they are paid workers or volunteers.

The voluntary sector

The *voluntary sector* includes organisations with non-charitable objectives but which are not-for-profit, independent, voluntarily-managed, and serving a community benefit. We have not discussed separately friendly or provident societies, religious organisations and private schools.

Boards or Committees

We have used the term *Committee* throughout the report to describe any management committee, board or executive committee whose members have ultimate legal responsibility for an organisation, whether unincorporated or a company limited by guarantee. The terminology can be confusing since charity trustees sometimes assign the day-to-day management to a management or executive committee whose members may not actually be trustees themselves. This can happen with the local branches of some charities where the branch is not autonomous. In these cases the committee is not legally responsible for the conduct of the organisation since its members are not trustees. Only the charity trustees bear full legal responsibility for its conduct.

Governance

Governance is the overall guidance, direction and supervision of the organisation.

Trustees

The term *trustee* normally refers to anyone exercising a governance role and responsible for the general control and management of a charity.

Holding or *custodian* trustees have a more limited function of holding the assets and investments of a charity for safe-keeping. They should not be confused with charity trustees.

Honorary Officers – for example the *Chair, Vice-Chair, Treasurer* – may be expected to carry out certain duties and exercise leadership, but all trustees share equally the same responsibilities towards the charity.

In view of the relevance of our report to a voluntary organisation without charitable status, we use *trustee* to include anyone who has overall responsibility for the governance of a voluntary organisation, whether charitable or otherwise, unless indicated in the text.

Finally, our discussion of trustees may be taken to have wider relevance to all those, not in charities, who receive in trust resources to be applied for the benefit of others.

Appendix 1: Those giving oral or written evidence

Those who gave oral evidence

Elizabeth Anionwu, Sickle Cell Society (trustee)

Walter Baker, South London Business Executive

Joan Davis, National Federation of Women's Institutes (trustee)

Chris Frost, Merton Council for Voluntary Service

Roger Harrison, Open University Community Education Department

Peter Houghton, Consultant

Mike Hudson, Compass Partnership

Paul Jackson, Comic Relief (trustee)

Heather Mayall, National Federation of Women's Institutes

Janet Morgan, Sainsbury Family Charitable Trusts

Michael Norton, Directory of Social Change

Elizabeth Shepherd, Hull Federation of Community Organisations (trustee)

Doug Simpson, Action with Communities in Rural England

Harold Sumption, Consultant (and trustee)

Dorcas Ward, Housing Corporation

Seven projects funded through the Advancing Good Management Scheme

Note: A number of those who gave oral evidence also made written submissions.

Those invited but unable to attend

Kate Cornell, National Federation of Housing Associations

Michael Gahagan, Doe Inner Cities Directorate

Joel Joffe, Allied Dunbar

Lord Pitt

Those interviewed by members of the Working Party

Tessa Baring, Chair of Barnardo's

Stephen Campbell, Association of County Councils

Harry Cayton, Alzheimers Disease Society

Nicholas Hinton, Save the Children Fund

Ray Husain, MIND

Sylvia Limerick, Chair of British Red Cross

Gordon Lishman, Age Concern England

Jo Lucas, MIND

Andrew Patterson, Association of Independent Museums

Nicholas Ridley, Association of Independent Museums (trustee)

Stuart Wallace, Adviser to the Association of District Councils

Peter Westland, Association of Metropolitan Associations

Michael Whitlam, British Red Cross

Note: A number of those interviewed also made written submissions.

Those who submitted written evidence

Sandy Adirondack, Consultant

Nancy Axelrod, National Center for Non-Profit Boards (USA)

Steve Balkam, Consultant

Arthur Brill, British Institute of Management

Kathy Cash, Royal National Institute for the Blind

Charlie Cattell, Industrial and Common Ownership Movement

Susanna Cheal, Consultant and Trustee

Richard Gibbs, Derbyshire Rural Community Council

Lindsay Driscoll, NCVO Legal Team

Sheila Evers, British Institute of Management

Rosemary Ewles, Museums and Gallery Commission

Jim Flood, Bradford Federation of Voluntary Management Committees

Kevin Ford, Framework

Geoff Fordham Associates, Consultants Inner Cities Unit, Department of Trade and Industry

Sir William Goodhart, Queen's Council

Margaret Harris, Centre for Voluntary Organisation, London School of Economics

David Hobman, Charities Effectiveness Review Trust

Olga Johnson, Charity Recruitment

Alastair Kent, Action for Blind People
Linda Laurance, Chair of the Charity Forum
Stephen Lloyd, Bates, Wells & Braithwaite
Geoffrey Lord, Carnegie Trust
Rosemary Marsh, British Association of Friends of Museums
Kim Maxwell, Association of Community Trusts and Foundations
Sheila McKechnie, Shelter
Foster Murphy, Volunteer Centre UK
Graham Mussell, Alexander Stenhouse UK Ltd
John Norton, BDO Binder Hamlyn and NSPCC treasurer
Ania Oprawska, Action Resource Centre
Shirley Otto, Consultant
Andrew Phillips, Bates, Wells & Braithwaite
Richard Radcliffe, Buzzacott
Jane Raimes, Community Council for Dorset
Alec Reed, The Trustee Register
Josephine Seccombe, Consultant
Bernard Spiegal, London Adventure Playground Association
Anne Stamper, Royal Society of Arts Diploma
Guy Stringer, International Fund-Raising Workshop
Phil Turner, Common Knowledge
Terry Veich, Charity Recruitment
Lin Whitfield, Action Resource Centre (Bristol)
Louise Wilby, Royal Society for Nature Conservation
David Wilcox, Partnership
Michael Coop, Bacon and Woodrow
Nicholas Young, British Red Cross

In addition valuable written submissions were made by a number of members of the Working Party at different stages.

Appendix 2: Suggested reading

This list contains a selection of publications available to trustees to support their work.

General

Dayton, Kenneth. *Governance is Governance*, Oakleaf Foundation (US), 1987

George, Peter. *Making Charities Effective*, a guide for charities and voluntary bodies, Jessica Kingsley, 1989

Houle, Cyril O. *Governing Boards: Their Nature and Nurture*, National Center for Non-Profit Boards (US), 1989

O'Connell. *The Board Members Book*, Foundation Centre (US), 1985

Philips, Andrew. *Charitable Status*, Interchange, 1988

Role of Committee members

CAF. *The Duties and Personal Liabilities of Charity Trustees*, Charities Aid Foundation, 1991

National Center for Non-Profit Boards Governance Series (US), 1990. Booklets 1–7 covering responsibilities and tasks of board members

Fenton, Lawrence. *The Hon Treasurer – Charities and Voluntary Organisations*, Institute of Chartered Accountants, 1980

How Is It Going? Personal and organisational review for members of management committees of voluntary organisations, Open University, 1990

SCVS. *Committees Workpack*, Scottish Council for Voluntary Organisations (undated)

NCVO Practical Guides series

Baine, Sean, Benington, John and Russell, Jill. *Changing Europe: Challenges Facing the Voluntary and Community Sectors in the 1990s*, NCVO Publications, 1992

Capper, Sally. *But Is It Legal? Fundraising and the Law*, NCVO Publications, 1988

Capper, Sally. *Starting and Running a Voluntary Group*, NCVO Publications, 1989

Clarke, Steve. *Seeing It Through: How to Be Effective on a Committee*, NCVO Publications and Community Development Foundation, 1989

Davison, Ann and Seary, Bill. *Grants from Europe: How to Get Money and Influence Policy*, 1991

Feek, Warren. *Working Effectively: A Guide to Evaluation Techniques*, 1988

Harvey, Brian. *Networking in Europe: A Guide to European Voluntary Organisations*, NCVO Publications, 1992

Hutt, Jane. *Opening the Town Hall Door: An Introduction to Local Government*, NCVO Publications, 1989

Jones, Maggie. *Using the Media*, NCVO Publications, 1992

Marlow, Joyce. *Industrial Tribunals and Appeals: Everything You Need to Know*, NCVO Publications, 1991

Sikking, Maggi. *Organising Your Finance: A Guide to Good Practice*, NCVO Publications, 1987

Many other organisations have useful handbooks including: the Law Centres Federation, British Red Cross, St John Ambulance, Motor Neurone Disease Association and Age Concern England's Management Development Unit.

Charity Commission leaflets

Acquiring Land, CC33

Capital Expenditure by Charity Trustees, CC38

Charities Act 1992, HMSO

Charities Acts 1960 and 1985: Charity Accounts, CC25

Charities and Local Authorities, CC29

Charity Accounts: Notes for charity trustees, AC7

The Charity Commissioners: How they can help charity trustees, CC2

Fundraising and Charities, CC20

Making a Scheme, CC36

Official Custodian for Charities: Investment management by charity trustees, CC14

Payment of Charity Trustees, CC41

Political Activities by Charities, CC9

Responsibilities of Charity Trustees, CC3

Selling Charity Land, CC28

Organisation and management

Adirondack, Sandy Merritt. *Just about Managing*, London Voluntary Service Council, 1989

Allen, G and Houghton, P. *The Fifth Estate: People and Power in Associations*, European Society of Association Executives, 1990

ACRE. ACRE Newsletter for Charity Trustees: *Local Charity*, biannual

Cairns, Elizabeth. *Charities: Law and Practice*, Sweet and Maxwell, 1988

The Charity Finance Director's Handbook, Letts and Co, 1991

Croner's Management of Voluntary Organisations, Croner Publications. A loose-leaf reference service with quarterly updates

Diamond, A.V.M. et al. *Charities Administration: A Manual of Effective Organisation and Practice*, Institute of Chartered Secretaries and Administrators, updated annually

Feek, Warren. *Management Committees: Practising Community Control*, National Youth Agency, 1982

Forbes, D., Hayes, R. and Reason, J. *Voluntary But Not Amateur: A Guide to the Law for Voluntary and Community Groups*, London Voluntary Service Council, 1990

Gawlinski, George and Graessle, Lois. *Planning Together: The Art of Effective Teamwork*, NCVO Publications, 1988

Graessle, Lois and Ly Ung, Van. *Methods for Managing: A Handbook for Community Associations of Refugees from Vietnam*. Refugee Action, 1990

Handy, Charles. *Understanding Voluntary Organisations*, Penguin, 1988

Harris, Margaret. *Management Committees in Practice: A Study in Local Voluntary Leadership*, Working Paper No 7, The Centre for Voluntary Organisations, London School of Economics, 1989

Housing Corporation. *Performance Expectations: Housing Association Committee Members' Guide to Self-Monitoring*, Housing Corporation, 1989

Ireland, Minna. *Horns & Halos: Management Issues Facing Local Voluntary Organisations*, Cleveland Associations for Management in Voluntary Organisations, 1990

Jones, H. (ed) *Members' Handbook: Boards of Visitors*, Association of Members of Boards of Visitors, 1991

Kalpana, Joshi and Maxwell, Kim. *Foundations for Community Trusts*, Association of Community Trusts and Foundations, 1992

Michaels, Maurice. *Training Needs of Synagogue Leadership: Identification and Acceptance*, Leo Baeck College, 1990

NCVO. Specimen Deed of Charitable Trust, Specimen Constitution for an Unincorporated Association Having Membership (Seeking Charitable Status), Specimen Memorandum of Association for a Company Limited by Guarantee (Having Charitable Status), and Specimen Articles of Association for a Company Limited by Guarantee (Having Charitable Status), available from NCVO Legal Department

NFCO, *Goalposts Moving for Voluntary Organisations: Urgency of Voluntary Management Training*, National Federation of Community Organisations, 1992

NFWI. *Any Other Business: A Guide to Running a Women's Institute*, National Federation of Women's Institutes, undated

Otto, Shirley and Holloway, Christine, *Getting Organised: A Handbook for Non-Statutory Organisations*, NCVO Publications, 1985

Scottish Arts Council. *Care, Diligence and Skill: A Handbook for the Governing Bodies of Arts Organisations*, Scottish Arts Council, 1987

Thornton, Christine. *Managing to Advise*, Federation of Independent Advice Centres, 1989

Tolley's Charities Manual, Tolley Publishing Co Ltd, 1991. Loose-leaf publication regularly updated.

Index